THE
POTAWATOMI

THE
POTAWATOMI

James A. Clifton
University of Wisconsin, Green Bay

Frank W. Porter III
General Editor

CHELSEA HOUSE PUBLISHERS
New York   Philadelphia

On the cover   A Potawatomi beaded sash

Editor-in-Chief   Nancy Toff
Executive Editor   Remmel T. Nunn
Managing Editor   Karyn Gullen Browne
Copy Chiefs   Perry Scott King, Juli Barbato
Art Director   Giannella Garrett
Picture Editor   Juliette Dickstein

Staff for THE POTAWATOMI

Senior Editor   Marjorie P. K. Weiser
Associate Editor   Andrea E. Reynolds
Senior Designer   Laurie Jewell
Design Assistant   Laura Lang
Copy Editors   Sean Dolan, Gillian Bucky,
                 Ellen Scordato
Picture Research   Susan B. Hamburger
Production Coordinator   Alma Rodriguez

Creative Director   Harold Steinberg

3   5   7   9   8   6   4   2

Library of Congress Cataloging-in-Publication Data

Clifton, James A.
The Potawatomi.

(Indians of North America)
Bibliography: p.
Includes index.
Summary: Examines the history, changing fortunes, and current situation
of the Potawatomi Indians. Includes a picture essay on their crafts.
1. Potawatomi Indians. [1. Potawatomi Indians. 2. Indians of North
America] I. Porter, Frank W., 1947–   . II. Title. III. Series: Indians of
North America (Chelsea House Publishers)
E99.P8C547   1987   970.004'97   87-5170

ISBN 1-55546-725-3
    0-7910-0366-3 (pbk.)

CONTENTS

INDIANS OF NORTH AMERICA

CHELSEA HOUSE PUBLISHERS

INDIANS OF NORTH AMERICA: CONFLICT AND SURVIVAL

Frank W. Porter III

*The Indians survived our
open intention of wiping them
out, and since the tide turned
they have even weathered
our good intentions toward them,
which can be much more deadly.*

John Steinbeck
America and Americans

When Europeans first reached the North American continent, they found hundreds of tribes occupying a vast and rich country. The newcomers quickly recognized the wealth of natural resources. They were not, however, so quick or willing to recognize the spiritual, cultural, and intellectual riches of the people they called Indians.

The Indians of North America examines the problems that develop when people with different cultures come together. For American Indians, the consequences of their interaction with non-Indian people have been both productive and tragic. The Europeans believed they had "discovered" a "New World," but their religious bigotry, cultural bias, and materialistic world view kept them from appreciating and understanding the people who lived in it. All too often they attempted to change the way of life of the indigenous people. The Spanish conquistadores wanted the Indians as a source of labor. The Christian missionaries, many of whom were English, viewed them as potential converts. French traders and trappers used the Indians as a means to obtain pelts. As Francis Parkman, the 19th-century historian, stated, "Spanish civilization crushed the Indian; English civilization scorned and neglected him; French civilization embraced and cherished him."

Nearly 500 years later, many people think of American Indians as curious vestiges of a distant past, waging a futile war to survive in a Space Age society. Even today, our understanding of the history and culture of American Indians is too often derived from unsympathetic, culturally biased, and inaccurate reports. The American Indian, described and portrayed in thousands of movies, television programs, books, articles, and government studies, has either been raised to the status of the "noble savage" or disparaged as the "wild Indian" who resisted the westward expansion of the American frontier.

Where in this popular view are the real Indians, the human beings and communities whose ancestors can be traced back to ice-age hunters? Where are the creative and indomitable people whose sophisticated technologies used the natural resources to ensure their survival, whose military skill might even have prevented European settlement of North America if not for devastating epidemics and the disruption of the ecology? Where are the men and women who are today diligently struggling to assert their legal rights and express once again the value of their heritage?

The various Indian tribes of North America, like people everywhere, have a history that includes population expansion, adaptation to a range of regional environments, trade across wide networks, internal strife, and warfare. This was the reality. Europeans justified their conquests, however, by creating a mythical image of the New World and its native people. In this myth, the New World was a virgin land, waiting for the Europeans. The arrival of Christopher Columbus ended a timeless primitiveness for the original inhabitants.

Also part of this myth was the debate over the origins of the American Indians. Fantastic and diverse answers were proposed by the early explorers, missionaries, and settlers. Some thought that the Indians were descended from the Ten Lost Tribes of Israel, others that they were descended from inhabitants of the lost continent of Atlantis. One writer suggested that the Indians had reached North America in another Noah's ark.

A later myth, perpetrated by many historians, focused on the relentless persecution during the past five centuries until only a scattering of these "primitive" people remained to be herded onto reservations. This view fails to chronicle the overt and covert ways in which the Indians successfully coped with the intruders.

All of these myths presented one-sided interpretations that ignored the complexity of European and American events and policies. All left serious questions unanswered. What were the origins of the American Indians? Where did they come from? How and when did they get to the New World? What was their life—their culture—really like?

In the late 1800s, anthropologists and archaeologists in the Smithsonian Institution's newly created Bureau of American Ethnology in Washington, D. C., began to study scientifically the history and culture of the Indians of North America. They were motivated by an honest belief that the Indians were on the verge of extinction and that along with them would vanish their languages, religious beliefs, technology, myths, and legends. These men and women went out to visit, study, and record data from as many Indian communities as possible before this information was forever lost.

8

By this time there was a new myth in the national consciousness. American Indians existed as figures in the American past. They had performed a historical mission. They had challenged white settlers who trekked across the continent. Once conquered, however, they were supposed to accept graciously the way of life of their conquerors.

The reality again was different. American Indians resisted both actively and passively. They refused to lose their unique identity, to be assimilated into white society. Many whites viewed the Indians not only as members of a conquered nation but also as "inferior" and "unequal." The rights of the Indians could be expanded, contracted, or modified as the conquerors saw fit. In every generation, white society asked itself what to do with the American Indians. Their answers have resulted in the twists and turns of federal Indian policy.

There were two general approaches. One way was to raise the Indians to a "higher level" by "civilizing" them. Zealous missionaries considered it their Christian duty to elevate the Indian through conversion and scanty education. The other approach was to ignore the Indians until they disappeared under pressure from the ever-expanding white society. The myth of the "vanishing Indian" gave stronger support to the latter option, helping to justify the taking of the Indians' land.

Prior to the end of the 18th century, there was no national policy on Indians simply because the American nation had not yet come into existence. American Indians similarly did not possess a political or social unity with which to confront the various Europeans. They were not homogeneous. Rather, they were loosely formed bands and tribes, speaking nearly 300 languages and thousands of dialects. The collective identity felt by Indians today is a result of their common experiences of defeat and/or mistreatment at the hands of whites.

During the colonial period, the British crown did not have a coordinated policy toward the Indians of North America. Specific tribes (most notably the Iroquois and the Cherokee) became military and political pawns used by both the crown and the individual colonies. The success of the American Revolution brought no immediate change. When the United States acquired new territory from France and Mexico in the early 19th century, the federal government wanted to open this land to settlement by homesteaders. But the Indian tribes that lived on this land had signed treaties with European governments assuring their title to the land. Now the United States assumed legal responsibility for honoring these treaties.

At first, President Thomas Jefferson believed that the Louisiana Purchase contained sufficient land for both the Indians and the white population.

Within a generation, though, it became clear that the Indians would not be allowed to remain. In the 1830s the federal government began to coerce the eastern tribes to sign treaties agreeing to relinquish their ancestral land and move west of the Mississippi River. Whenever these negotiations failed, President Andrew Jackson used the military to remove the Indians. The southeastern tribes, promised food and transportation during their removal to the West, were instead forced to walk the "Trail of Tears." More than 4,000 men, women, and children died during this forced march. The "removal policy" was successful in opening the land to homesteaders, but it created enormous hardships for the Indians.

By 1871 most of the tribes in the United States had signed treaties ceding most or all of their ancestral land in exchange for reservations and welfare. The treaty terms were intended to bind both parties for all time. But in the General Allotment Act of 1887, the federal government changed its policy again. Now the goal was to make tribal members into individual landowners and farmers, encouraging their absorption into white society. This policy was advantageous to whites who were eager to acquire Indian land, but it proved disastrous for the Indians. One hundred thirty-eight million acres of reservation land were subdivided into tracts of 160, 80, or as little as 40 acres, and allotted to tribe members on an individual basis. Land owned in this way was said to have "trust status" and could not be sold. But the surplus land—all Indian land not allotted to individuals— was opened (for sale) to white settlers. Ultimately, more than 90 million acres of land were taken from the Indians by legal and illegal means.

The resulting loss of land was a catastrophe for the Indians. It was necessary to make it illegal for Indians to sell their land to non-Indians. The Indian Reorganization Act of 1934 officially ended the allotment period. Tribes that voted to accept the provisions of this act were reorganized, and an effort was made to purchase land within preexisting reservations to restore an adequate land base.

Ten years later, in 1944, federal Indian policy again shifted. Now the federal government wanted to get out of the "Indian business." In 1953 an act of Congress named specific tribes whose trust status was to be ended "at the earliest possible time." This new law enabled the United States to end unilaterally, whether the Indians wished it or not, the special status that protected the land in Indian tribal reservations. In the 1950s federal Indian policy was to transfer federal responsibility and jurisdiction to state governments, encourage the physical relocation of Indian peoples from reservations to urban areas, and hasten the termination, or extinction, of tribes.

Between 1954 and 1962 Congress passed specific laws authorizing the termination of more than 100 tribal groups. The stated purpose of the termination policy was to ensure the full and complete integration of Indians into American society. However, there is a less benign way to interpret this legislation. Even as termination was being discussed in Congress, 133 separate bills were introduced to permit the transfer of trust land ownership from Indians to non-Indians.

With the Johnson administration in the 1960s the federal government began to reject termination. In the 1970s yet another Indian policy emerged. Known as "self-determination," it favored keeping the protective role of the federal government while increasing tribal participation in, and control of, important areas of local government. In 1983 President Reagan, in a policy statement on Indian affairs, restated the unique "government to government" relationship of the United States with the Indians. However, federal programs since then have moved toward transferring Indian affairs to individual states, which have long desired to gain control of Indian land and resources.

As long as American Indians retain power, land, and resources that are coveted by the states and the federal government, there will continue to be a "clash of cultures," and the issues will be contested in the courts, Congress, the White House, and even in the international human rights community. To give all Americans a greater comprehension of the issues and conflicts involving American Indians today is a major goal of this series. These issues are not easily understood, nor can these conflicts be readily resolved. The study of North American Indian history and culture is a necessary and important step toward that comprehension. All Americans must learn the history of the relations between the Indians and the federal government, recognize the unique legal status of the Indians, and understand the heritage and cultures of the Indians of North America.

*All Neshnabe boys, and some girls, went into the wilderness on
a vision quest to get a personal spirit guardian to help them
throughout life. Even today Potawatomi young people may seek
a vision to guide their future lives.*

POTAWATOMI GENESIS

In the beginning, the Old People taught, there was no land, only water. Floating on this Great Sea was a birchbark canoe. In it, weeping, sat a man, Our Grandfather. He wept because he had no idea of his fate.

After a time Chief Muskrat appeared and climbed into the canoe. "Grandfather," he asked, "why are you crying so?"

"I weep because I have been here a long, long while, and there is no land," the man replied.

"But there is Earth down deep under the Great Sea," responded Muskrat. "If you wish, I can swim down and bring some back to you." Our Grandfather nodded, "Yes."

Muskrat disappeared beneath the Great Sea and then bobbed up again, a gob of Earth in his mouth. "Are you alone like me?" asked Our Grandfather.

"No," replied Chief Muskrat, and he called to his fellows, the other chiefs of the animals who dwelled in the waters. They appeared, one by one.

First came Beaver, then Snapping Turtle, then Otter. Each in turn dove deep into the Great Sea and then reappeared, bearing a ball of Earth clenched in his mouth.

From these gobs of Earth, explained the Old People, Our Grandfather fashioned This Island. Day after day he added to it as his Grandchildren brought more Earth, until it was large enough and solidly anchored in the Great Sea. Then he planted the Great Tree and other growing things. Using a stick, he marked out the rivers and had the muskrats dig out their channels. But he was still alone, was Our Grandfather, he whom we call Master of All Life, *Wiske* (WIS kay).

One day, still alone, Wiske walked toward the north of Our Island. There he met some humans, naked and poor, who told him they were the *Neshnabek*, the True People. "Who are you?" the Neshnabek called. "I am the Master of All Life," he replied. "I will create everything you need. I will teach you

A floor mat woven of rushes. Wiske taught the People how to weave rush mats, and all other things they needed to know.

how to lead a decent, good life."

And so Wiske taught the True People. He gave them knowledge of how to make and use bark canoes, pottery, bows and arrows, bark and rush-mat covered wigwams—everything they needed. He showed them what animals and plants were good to eat, and how to prepare them. He taught them how to plant and harvest corn, beans, and squash. The Neshnabek learned fast.

The Master of All Life also taught the People how to lead the Good Life. From him they learned to divide themselves into families, villages, and clans, each with its own *wkama* (w' KAH ma), or chief. The People now understood that they must keep peace among themselves, never shedding the blood of another Neshnabe. What was proper for Man and what for Woman, Wiske taught them. He taught that no Neshnabe must ever hold power over the affairs of any other. No one should ever accumulate wealth beyond what others owned.

For the Neshnabek to worship, Wiske gave them their Sacred Bundles, which they called *Pitchkosan*, "Watches Over Us." Each Sacred Bundle contained the special powers of the village or clan to which it belonged. Wiske also taught the People all the rituals they must observe, all the special knowledge they needed to protect themselves, and the importance of dreams and visions.

But Wiske had a twin, *Chipiyapos*, as different from him as summer from winter. Chipiyapos did not create, he destroyed. He was a tricky, deceitful, devilish being. He brought the Neshnabek disunity, misbehavior, troubles, and finally Death. Chipiyapos is keeper of the afterworld, beyond the far rim of Our Island, the place where all Neshnabek must go one day. And he looks so like Wiske that the People can never be certain which is the Good One, which the Evil.

This version of the People's sacred account of their creation is much abbreviated. The original takes many hours to tell in full. It represents the Neshnabek's understanding of part of their history, dating from a time when they were one people, independent, with a single language and culture.

They had many other such creation or origin myths. Each clan had its own legend of how a founder had a vision and was given the special power to create a new *dodem* (clan). There were also many other tales explaining important matters: why women should not be chiefs, for example, or how the People got horses. All these myths and legends served the People in important ways.

Other American Indians had similar creation myths. This particular myth pattern occurs so often that it has been named the Earth Diver myth, after the animals who dive beneath the sea, bringing up bits of dirt to help create the world. The myth's central figure, Wiske, is an example of a culture hero.

The myths and legends that the Old People told to the young were rich with symbolism. Like their culture hero Wiske, we have to look beneath the surface to find the substance, the lessons in them. The origin myth, for instance, expresses the Neshnabek's feelings of importance: They were the first, true, chosen humans. It explains much: where the sun goes, the shape of the earth—an Island in the Great Sea—how the world began, and how the People acquired their culture or way of life.

But creation myths go deeper, to an understanding of human nature. Read closely and you will discover how the Neshnabek understood human nature. In the beginning the People were naked and poor—without culture. Until they met the Master Of All Life, a teacher with special powers, they lacked skills, knowledge, and even morals. Humans, the Neshnabek believed, were weak creatures until they found a superna-

Sacred Bundles, used by their owners in special clan ceremonies, were made out of animal skins. Bottom: *otter skin bundle with porcupine quill decoration;* top right: *mink skin bundle with cloth and silk ornaments;* top left: *bundle made from the head and neck of a bald eagle.*

tural guardian. Wiske thus became the protector of all Neshnabek.

At the age of about 11 or 12 years, each individual Neshnabe had to go out into the wilderness alone and naked, without food or drink. After a while, each would receive a vision and acquire a personal spirit guardian. Each personal spirit helper, the Neshnabek believed, was also Wiske, appearing in one or another of his many shapes and identities. All Neshnabek boys, and some girls, had to go on such a vision quest.

Throughout their history the beliefs of the People always influenced how they would react to events and changing circumstances. But, as their myths show, the People were of two minds about their condition.

The origin myth explains that in the beginning the Neshnabek were weak and helpless. But they did not like this and always worked to improve their condition. Obtaining a supernatural helper was one way to do this. Wiske had shown the way to the Good Life, but his other side, his twin Chipiyapos, expressed the dark, evil side of human nature. The People tried to live together in harmony, but they anticipated danger and immorality. Their lives were guided by high ideals, but they faced a hard reality.

A different, less poetic early history of the Neshnabek comes from archaeological research, the evidence of linguistics (the study of languages), and the reports of early European visitors to the Great Lakes area. We know that before A.D. 1500 their ancestors lived north of Lakes Huron and Superior. In their language, culture, and social life, they were then much like the small, closely related bands of Ojibwa (Chippewa) and Ottawa who lived nearby.

At about A.D. 1500 the Neshnabek migrated south and settled in a warmer climate along the lower eastern shore of Lake Michigan. Within a century they established some dozen villages, from what is now Ludington in the north to St. Joseph in the south.

They brought with them many skills, such as hunting, fishing, and the gathering of natural plant foods. These skills required extensive knowledge of the plant and animal life of the environment and formed the basis of their subsistence activities, the ways in

An Indian snowshoe. Snowshoes tied onto moccasins make it easy to walk across deep snow.

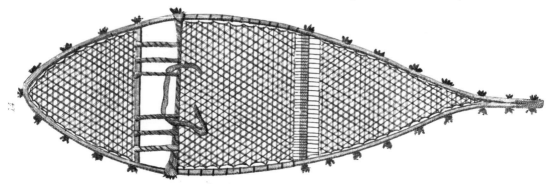

Nampizha, the underwater horned panther who is part human, is engraved on a shell worn on a beaded neckband.

which they supported themselves.

People who live in the same way as these ancient Neshnabek are known as foragers. Foraging peoples must go out to collect and gather from their environment the necessities of their lives, as these resources occur naturally, each in its season. Women were primarily responsible for gathering vegetable foods; they also assisted with fishing. The men's primary responsibilities were hunting and the heavy work of fishing. Seasonal foraging requires that people move frequently, from fall to winter to spring, as well as from one year to the next, to allow time for the plant and animal resources to be replenished. When they lived north of the Great Lakes, the Neshnabek had been seasonally nomadic foragers.

The Neshnabek also brought with them from the north their technology, especially their means of transportation. For winter travel they made and used snowshoes and toboggans. For long distance travel in warm weather, the People built and used lightweight, carefully framed canoes sheathed with birch bark.

Because bark canoes are fragile, easily pierced by unseen snags or swamped in rough waters, the Neshnabek were wary sailors. No sensible True Human would travel out of sight of land or in bad weather. No one would set foot in a canoe until the leader of the trip had made an offering. He had to cast some tobacco into the water to appease *Nampizha*. This creature—part horned panther, part human—lurked there, ready to trap and drown any unwary Neshnabek.

Once the Neshnabek settled along Lake Michigan's shores, their canoes gave them an advantage over their new neighbors, the Sac, Fox, and Kickapoo. None of these tribes knew how to build or navigate bark canoes, but they did have other skills and knowledge that would soon be useful to the People.

In the warmer climate to which they moved, the Neshnabek found lush new hunting and fishing grounds. Deer, their main game animal, were plentiful. There were also large herds of elk and, in the rich prairies nearby, buffalo.

From their new neighbors they learned of a revolutionary way of sub-

A herd of buffalo moving across the plains.

sisting. The Sac and Fox gave the People the skills, knowledge, and seeds necessary to cultivate and harvest corn, beans, and squash. This transformed their economy. They became food producers, not simply food collectors.

Thus, shortly after settling in Michigan, the People added horticulture to their old foraging techniques. Horticulture, as anthropologists use the word, means human-powered farming. Because there were no large animals suitable for domestication in North America, ancient farm work on this continent used human muscle power.

The phrase "human-powered farming" is somewhat misleading. The daily responsibility of laboring amidst the hills of corn, beans, and squash was woman's work. And important work it was, since the labor of women added a greatly increased supply of valuable new vegetable foods. By farming the women could provide more vegetable food than they could by foraging. Soon the farms of the Neshnabek women were supplying more than half the food consumed in their villages. They frequently produced surpluses of corn and squash. These new foods were dried and stored for later use, making life more secure. These surpluses could also be used for trade.

Because they produced the profitable surplus foods, the position of women in Neshnabek life began to change. Their new economic roles made them even more important than when the ancestral Neshnabek were northern foragers.

After the Neshnabek became horticulturists in Michigan, their population increased and they adopted a more settled life. They became seasonally

THE
ANTHROPOLOGIST
MEETS THE
POTAWATOMI

I first met the Potawatomi, as they are called by Americans, in Kansas in September 1962. That first encounter was accidental. I was a young anthropologist teaching at the University of Kansas, looking for a place where students could learn to do research in a culturally distinct community.

I soon learned that, when speaking their own language, they called themselves *Neshnabek*. This means, simply, the People, in the sense of True People or Genuine Humans, as against everyone else. For this reason, I sometimes speak of them as Neshnabek, as they were in the beginning, or the People, as well as Potawatomi. How they acquired the latter name is part of their history.

Similarly, the Neshnabek first called me the *Kitchimokomon*, which means the Big Knife. This is what they have always called Americans. When speaking their language, they do not use words meaning white man, since like other American Indians they were never much concerned with the color of anyone's skin. To use such a racial label as "white" in this narrative would be a historical mistake. Thinking that divides the people of North America into white, red, or black "races" reflects the persistent confusion of Americans about culture and biology.

That September day was a complete surprise to me. On the sun-parched prairies north of Topeka, I disovered several hundred authentic Great Lakes area Indians busily engaged in an important harvest ritual. I started asking questions about them, as well as of them. How had these Wisconsin or Illinois Indians come to Kansas? What was this religious ceremony all about?

It is easy for an anthropologist to ask questions. Asking the right questions and getting answers to them are other matters. That would take much travel and many years. From Kansas to Iowa to Wisconsin and Michigan, then into Canada, Indiana, Illinois, and other places, I followed the historical trail of the Potawatomi. As I pursued them, I came to know the People as they were long ago and as they are today.

The Potawatomi of Kansas offered much hospitality and patience. Others, elsewhere, later did the same. What I learned would have been impossible without them.

sedentary, staying in one place, establishing large, durable villages near their cornfields. They left these villages only temporarily—during a long winter hunt, for example. They did have to move their villages every dozen years or so, when their crops had exhausted the nutrients in the soil, and when they had to travel too far to cut and carry firewood.

As their population increased, so too did the size of the villages. Since these communities were close to one another, the Neshnabek could now cooperate more often in larger groups, and so their social life changed as well. Eventually their social organization came to resemble that of the nearby Sac and Kickapoo.

They became a tribe, a society consisting of a dozen or so settled villages that regularly coordinated some of their important activities. This cooperation was managed by the *wkamek* (w' KAH mek), a council of elder leaders, each of whom represented a clan, some other group of kin, or a village. But they remained true to the moral lessons taught by Wiske, and no *wkama*, individual leader, held power over anyone. These leaders could suggest, encourage, or plead, but they could not command. The Neshnabek, wary of the dark side of human nature, watched their leaders carefully, ready to chastise or depose them if they got too ambitious.

A century after the Neshnabek left their ancient homeland in the north, their way of life was much changed. They had brought with them a tech-

nological advantage over their new neighbors, the construction and use of bark canoes. After they learned horticulture, they had new, larger, and more reliable supplies of food. This made possible a more sedentary life and a growing population. Now they were able to organize larger numbers of people for useful purposes: trade, war, and diplomacy.

About 1600 the Neshnabek began hearing strange rumors from people who had traveled to the east. These secondhand stories told of the arrival of unknown creatures who in some ways looked like humans, but dressed peculiarly, smelled bad, and—most surprising of all—had thick hair on their cheeks. These strange beings had new kinds of tools so valuable they were almost magical in their power. These beings the Neshnabek came to call the "Hairy Faces." In 1634 they had their first opportunity to meet one.

This was Jean Nicolet, who that summer traveled from the tiny French settlements along the St. Lawrence River to what is now Green Bay in Wisconsin. Nicolet was on a diplomatic mission to open the western Great Lakes to French trade. Some Neshnabek, hearing of the approach of this stranger, launched their canoes, and coasted along the northern rim of Lake Michigan. They journeyed to the meeting place at what is now Red Bank, on the Door Peninsula on the western shore of the lake.

It was then that the Neshnabek acquired a new name. When Nicolet first

An artist's impression of the Indians' meeting in 1634 with Jean Nicolet, the first French person or "Hairy Face" the Potawatomi ever saw.

saw them, he asked one of his guides, "Who are those people?" His guides, Huron Indians from Ontario, misunderstood and replied in their own language, "They are making a fire."

The Frenchman did not understand what the guides had said, but he wrote down their reply in French as *Pouutouatami*. Over the years this word was spelled in more than 50 different ways and finally standardized as Potawatomi. Nicolet thought it meant "the Firemakers." But it was not a word that meant anything to the Neshnabek in their own or any other language. So,

owing to a confusion in communication, the Neshnabek became known to others as the Potawatomi.

The People had no further contact with the French for several years. Back in their Michigan villages they faced grave threats, and these quickly occupied their full attention. By 1634 they had successfully completed the first leg of their Great Lakes odyssey, finding a new home and way of life in Michigan. But within a few years they were to become refugees, forced into a second migration, this one to a very different environment. ▲

A Potawatomi man of the mid-17th century holds French cloth and a knife, traded for furs. His hair is dressed in traditional fashion, powdered with red earth or ochre and threaded through bone and copper hair tubes or ornaments.

EXODUS
AND
REFUGE

After Nicolet's brief report, seven years passed before the People were again mentioned in the French chronicles. Then, in 1641, Jesuit missionaries heard reports that the Potawatomi were fleeing their Michigan lands and seeking asylum west of Lake Michigan.

This migration was not voluntary. A great panic was sweeping through the horticultural tribes of Michigan. Large armed parties had come from the East, bent on what the Jesuits called "wars of extermination." The invaders were a populous confederacy of Iroquoian tribes from the Ontario Peninsula. They were called the Neutrals by the French, because their territory was located between warring tribes. A few years later, devastating attacks by other Iroquois tribes, from New York—the Oneida, Cayuga, Mohawk, Seneca, and Onondaga—would in turn destroy the Neutrals and related tribes in Ontario, the Huron and Petun. Then, in the late 1650s, these New York Iroquois tribes, known as the Five Nations, expanded their assaults to include the tribes south of the Great Lakes.

By 1680 all the tribes of Ohio, Michigan, and northern Indiana and Illinois had been swept away. Where corn once stood tall and lush, weeds now grew. Wigwams had collapsed or burned. Bones littered the landscape. Those who survived the Iroquois onslaught were either taken captive or, like the Potawatomi, fled further west.

To avoid the full fury of the invaders, the Potawatomi escaped before they could be attacked. In their canoes they traveled north and west, finally settling on the islands and along the shores of Green Bay, west of Lake Michigan, in what is now Wisconsin. They were soon joined by their old neighbors, the Sac, Fox, and Kickapoo, as well as the Miami and other tribes fleeing the invaders.

The Potawatomi had gotten away largely unscathed, transporting much of their valuables in their canoes. They worked to establish themselves among the peoples who were already living in the Green Bay region, the Winnebago and the Menominee. They considerably outnumbered these older residents of Wisconsin. They arrived, moreover, as an intact, cooperating, tribal people.

These were substantial advantages, which the People soon exploited. By consensus, their leaders now determined a policy for the tribe. All agreed that the People would seek a position of prestige and influence among neighboring Indian communities, whether old residents or other refugees.

They soon had the opportunity to demonstrate their resolution and strength. In 1653 the New York Iroquois sent an army to destroy the refugees assembled in northeastern Wisconsin. Learning of their approach, the defenders gathered their forces. The Potawatomi were the largest contingent of defenders, with 400 of the 1,000 warriors. On the eastern shore of the Door Peninsula, they built a large, fortified village named *Mitchigami*, meaning "Great Lake," a Potawatomi word later appropriated by the Europeans.

Armed only with bows and arrows, lances, and clubs, the defenders faced

A War Bundle of a warrior or leader held sacred objects for ceremonies before battle. The club at left is carved in the shape of a musket stock; the other two have deer hoof rattles and represent the thunderbird.

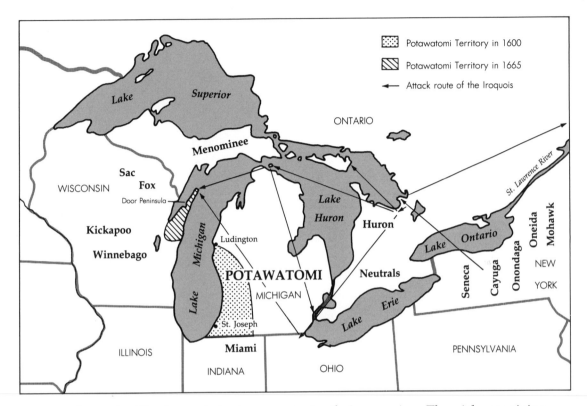

great hazards. The Iroquois had superior weapons, firearms acquired from the Dutch and English.

But the invaders had weaknesses, too. They were far from their home base, hungry and ill supplied, isolated in hostile territory. They faced courage and resolution, not panic, among the defenders. Moreover, the Potawatomi and their allies were well supplied, with enough food to withstand a siege.

The fortress at Mitchigami held firm. The invading Iroquois found it impregnable. Starving and unable to mount a lengthy siege, they agreed to a cease-fire. The defenders offered a feast in return—and fed poisoned corn

to their enemies. The sick, surviving Iroquois retreated, but the defenders pursued and nearly destroyed them. In later years the New York tribes twice repeated their attempt to conquer the refugee communities in Wisconsin. Both of these invasions failed as well, for the Potawatomi and their allies had made their refuge secure.

These events were episodes in the Beaver Wars, which had begun in the early 1640s in the east. The Iroquois and other eastern tribes were by now fully involved in a new form of trade with the French, English, and Dutch. The Indians' commodities were furs, which they exchanged for steel tools and weapons, firearms, woven cloth, glass beads, and other manufactured goods from Europe's workshops.

Of the furs, beaver was by far the most valuable to Europeans. Desirous of more trade, the eastern Indians quickly depleted the beaver supply in their own lands, and so the Iroquois set out to conquer and control new beaver-producing territory. For some time they were successful. Few tribes could stand fast against their persistent, well-armed, year-round onslaughts. But in the western Great Lakes they were stopped and decisively defeated by the Potawatomi and their allies. These confederates soon made the entire western Great Lakes region unsafe for Iroquois hunters and raiders.

To realize their tribal ambitions, though, the Potawatomi needed European allies and a regular supply of European trade goods and weapons. But the Iroquois still controlled the approaches to the French posts along the St. Lawrence River. This made traveling between the western lakes and the east hazardous and effectively cut off the People and their allies from contact with the French.

In the late 1660s the French at last established secure trading posts in the western Great Lakes. Their traders became more numerous, and soon emissaries of the French king arrived. Among them were licensed traders who had been given diplomatic responsibilities and Jesuit missionaries who served their order and faith as well as the French crown. Most prominent of the

French trapper-traders meeting an Indian, as imagined in this 19th-century engraving by Frederic Remington.

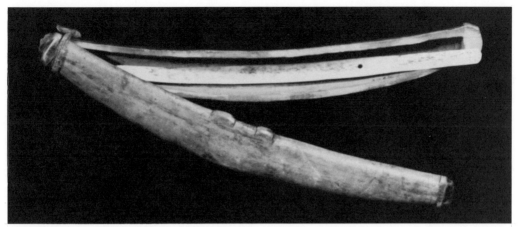

Potawatomi women used long needles carved from bone to sew clothing and other items. The needles were kept in a carved wooden case.

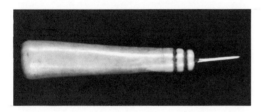

After they acquired metal by trading with Europeans, the Potawatomi were able to make tools like this awl, combining a metal point with a bone handle. This tool was used to make holes in animal skins so they could be sewn more easily.

traders was Nicholas Perrot, who spent many years with the People. Noteworthy among the missionaries was Father Claude Allouez.

The Potawatomi welcomed both men eagerly, for reasons of their own. The wkamek aimed to make the Potawatomi first among all the other tribes of the region. To impress the other tribes, they needed to display symbols of their own influence and to gain direct access to powerful French authorities. They wanted to establish themselves as brokers in the fur trade. Their plan was to obtain furs cheaply from more distant peoples and exchange them profitably for European goods.

They did not want to accumulate wealth, as the Europeans understood wealth. They expected that trading furs for European goods would bring them recognition, prestige, and influence among other tribes. Their leaders quickly saw that Father Allouez and Perrot could help them achieve these goals.

Of course the trader-diplomat and the missionary-diplomat had their own, entirely different plans. Perrot, especially, admired and was in turn greatly respected by the Potawatomi. They saw in him a means of gaining prosperity and with it great influence among neighboring tribes. They adopted him and named him *Mdamins* (Young Corn), a name they carefully selected to reflect the value they saw in him. Young corn was the most prized produce of their early autumn fields. When the corn was ripe came a time of plenty.

At first the wkamek told Nicholas Perrot, "Remain safely in our villages. We will send forth a *skabewis* (messenger) to speak on your behalf." When the astute Frenchman rejected this suggestion, the wkamek suggested an alternative: "If ·you must make such dangerous trips yourself, then we insist on providing bodyguards." Hence, as Perrot traveled about conducting his business, a large delegation of Potawatomi accompanied him, attending to their own affairs. Thus the Miami, Kickapoo, and others were made to understand that Perrot was a guest of the Potawatomi.

When Perrot finally became aware that the Potawatomi were scheming to become brokers in the fur trade, he provoked a confrontation. He was acting on firm instructions, he was loyal to the king and the governor of New France (as the French possessions of North America were known), and he was personally threatened. He and his French colleagues would be the principal brokers in the fur trade, not the Potawatomi elders.

In 1668 a great council of the tribe was held. The clan and village wkamek debated the French policies at length. They responded to Perrot's complaints diplomatically, with great unity, and decided on a mutually satisfactory compromise. One by one they stood and ritually chanted their agreement and commitment for this decision, for themselves and as representatives of their kin.

The elders agreed to welcome French traders into their villages and to aid and protect them. They agreed also to become active economic, political, and military allies of the French. Perrot, in turn, agreed that the French would help and supply the People, providing them with weapons and goods and making them the most favored tribe among all those of the western lakes. The Potawatomi were pleased. They had accomplished their goals.

The tribe's relationship with Claude Allouez would have somewhat different consequences. Eighteen months after Perrot's arrival, the Potawatomi eagerly sought out Allouez and invited him to live among them. They hoped the priest's presence and moral influence would subdue the carousing of rowdy French traders nearby. Allouez instead set out to make converts of the Indians. Luring the Potawatomi away from the strength and comforts of their traditional faith, his work threatened the integrity of their culture.

Allouez, like other missionaries, was not too successful. His message appealed to the elderly, to the seriously ill and dying, to small children, and occasionally to women. These few "conversions" were at best temporary and partial. Most of those who listened to his teachings reinterpreted his doctrines, recasting them into more familiar Potawatomi forms and meanings.

Their confidence in their own power, both political and supernatural, prevailed. The Potawatomi had entered into a long period of political success and economic plenty, and they remained content with their own religious leaders. Finally, the elders and warriors sent Allouez away. It would be decades before some Potawatomi lost enough confidence in their own ways to find an alien faith attractive.

The designs carved into this stick are a kind of picture writing intended to help a religious leader recall a sacred text during a ritual.

When they first heard of the French, the Potawatomi were sure that the "Hairy Faces" were supernatural creatures. When Perrot first came, they were surprised to see that he was shaped like a human, much like themselves except for his long beard. Nonetheless, they told him they believed he was a *Manidowkama*, a Spirit Chief, for he used iron tools and weapons. In part this was merely Potawatomi rhetoric, a way to honor and bedazzle their guest. They did, though, truly admire the superior technology of the newcomers.

They soon learned that the French, however different in language, ways, and appearance, were fully human in every way. These men with the bearded faces and steel knives and muskets got hungry, bled, and lusted like other men. The French, moreover, were all males. French women would not come to the western lake country for many years. The French traders lived among the tribes for years at a time. Because they had no women of their own, they sought mates from the Potawatomi and other native societies.

Potawatomi men soon recognized this as another opportunity. They were accustomed to exercising control over their daughters and sisters. Men normally decided whom the young women in their clans would marry. They arranged the marriages of daughters and sisters to make political and economic alliances and cement relationships with men from other clans, villages, and even tribes. Now they donated their young women as mates to French men.

This practice became known as "the custom of the country." Because the

Pipe stems, called calumets, were carried by men when they traveled. Any pipe bowl could be attached. The pipe bowls are made of steatite or pipestone, soft and easily carved when wet, but quite hard when dry. Calumets are made of wood, reed or bone.

Potawatomi had not accepted Christianity, French authorities and the Catholic church saw it as a casual and improper form of marriage. The Potawatomi men, however, believed they were creating strong, valuable, personal alliances with French traders, relationships secured by what they considered fully legitimate marriages to their daughters.

The children of these unions, however, were a different matter. By Potawatomi standards, a child born of a French man and a Potawatomi woman was an alien, not properly one of the People. The People were strongly patrilineal; membership in a clan, critical to the identity and welfare of all Potawatomi, was traced strictly through a line of males, all the way back to the mythological founder of the clan. Because the French fathers were not clan members, their children, and the grandchildren and great-grandchildren who came after them, could not inherit membership in a clan. They were not *nikdodem* (clanmates).

As the years passed and the "custom of the country" continued, there were more and more of these alien offspring living on the margin between Potawatomi and European life. These people were first called *brulés* (burned ones) or *métis* (mixed people) by the

A fire-making kit, used to kindle fires during ceremonies. The kit contains flints, a shaped steel for striking a spark, a bundle of tinder used to start a blaze, and a hawk wing to fan the flame.

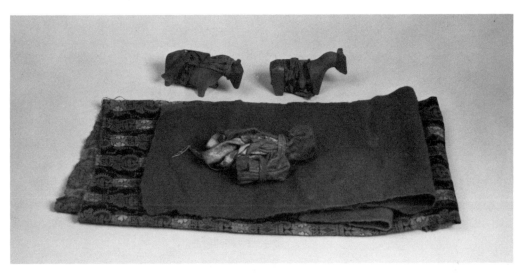

This Horse Medicine Bundle belonged to an individual. Its contents appeared to the owner in dreams: two carved wooden horses and three bags of colored earth paints, wrapped in European cloth.

French. To the Potawatomi, these marginals were not of their people at all. They were French or later *Sakonosh* (English). Even later they were *Kitchimokoman* (Big Knives), that is, Americans.

Beyond Potawatomi custom, practical problems were involved. The offspring of French, English, and, later, American men learned their fundamental customs, values, and ideals from their European fathers, not from their Indian mothers. Thus the children of these mixed marriages were a potential threat, a source of unwanted change in Potawatomi values and institutions.

The problem was all the greater because these children were rarely fully accepted in their fathers' home communities. As a result, an entirely new ethnic group developed, a people truly in between the Potawatomi and American communities. While the fur trade prospered, these marginal people were important in frontier society. When American agricultural settlement became predominant, the marginals—who were commonly called half-breeds or mixed-bloods by the English and Americans—became a serious problem to the Potawatomi.

Nevertheless, the alliance between the People and the French flourished for a century. Once securely established in the Wisconsin refuge area, bolstered and enriched by their French alliance, the Potawatomi population grew. Their economic and political successes and the rapid growth in their numbers were leading to the third part of their odyssey. ▲

A modern Potawatomi man wears a 19th-century costume and face paint of several different colors in parallel lines on his cheeks. This design, called Rainbow Road, indicates that he belongs to the Thunder Clan.

FLOWERING
OF THE
PEOPLE

The Green Bay area, rich in fish and game, was a particularly valuable location to both French and Indians. Here, safely distant from their Iroquois enemies, the Potawatomi found security. Whoever controlled Green Bay would also control the three major water routes between the French on the St. Lawrence and the interior of North America.

One route went from the bay down the Fox and Wisconsin rivers to the Mississippi. The second route went from Lake Michigan down the Chicago and Illinois rivers, also to the Mississippi. On the southeast side of the lake, in the Potawatomi's old homeland, lay the third route. This was the waterway from St. Joseph to the Kankakee and then the Illinois rivers, again leading to the Mississippi.

As French interests in the region prospered, so too did the economy and the prestige of the Potawatomi. Meanwhile, the French needed the Potawatomi as staunch allies against both Indian and British enemies.

The People's position in the Green Bay region was enhanced by several advantages. Among the first refugees to arrive in the area, they had also become more numerous than any other native society there. They brought with them, intact, a complete set of tribal institutions, which helped to coordinate the activities of their several communities. And they still had their technological advantages: the use of bark canoes and horticultural skills. As a result, the Potawatomi could provide the French with many trustworthy armed warriors, vital water transportation, ample supplies of food, secure havens in times of trouble, and bases for their operations.

By the 1670s the northeastern Wisconsin refuge area was becoming overpopulated. New arrivals and old residents were all competing for the same limited supply of natural resources, causing conflict. Meanwhile the Potawatomi's growing prosperity led to growth in their population, too. The 2,500 or so who had first migrated

from Michigan in 1641 would increase nearly fivefold, to about 12,000, by 1812.

The dense settlements of different tribes pushed many to consider new migrations. The Potawatomi started to move again in the 1680s. The expansion of French operations and the decline of the Iroquois menace made another migration both profitable and safe.

Potawatomi clan and village leaders could see much unoccupied land ready for the taking. Their first new settlements reached south to present-day Milwaukee. Then, in the last years of the decade, many traveled in their canoes back to their old homeland in

southwestern Michigan, along the St. Joseph River. By 1694 nearly 1,200 of them occupied that great valley.

The Potawatomi migrations were always group affairs. No individual or even family could conceive of going it alone or hope to survive isolated from kin. For the tribe to manage population and territorial expansion effectively and to be economically and politically successful, the People had to keep their basic institutions intact. All these objectives were accomplished through their clan system.

The Potawatomi dodem, or clan, was their most important social institution. Each dodem included not only its living members but also dead ancestors and people not yet born. Each had its own identity, symbols, rituals, special privileges, and property. Every Potawatomi belonged to one clan, and a person's membership and position in a clan was inherited through a line of male ancestors. Wherever they lived, *nikdodem* (clanmates) were considered closely related. Those in the same generation considered each other brothers and sisters, even if they did not have the same parents. Thus a person could not marry within the clan; each had to have a spouse from a different dodem. A man lived in a community with other members of his clan. After marriage, a woman retained membership in her own clan, but went to live with her husband. She was a stranger in the community of another clan.

The Potawatomi organized their population and territorial expansion by dividing their existing clans. The original Great Sea dodem, for instance, divided into the Fish, Sturgeon, Turtle, Frog, and Crab clans. As population grew and more migrations took place, the new clans would also divide. Thus the Sucker clan, which had split off from the Fish clan, later was subdivided into Golden, Red, and Black Sucker branches. When a new clan was formed, its members settled elsewhere, still keeping close ties to the founding dodem.

The members of a clan depended on one another for support throughout their lives. The dodem, like a modern corporation, was considered to be an individual. A blow struck against any one *Mozo*, Moose, was an injury to all members of the Moose clan, calling for retaliation and revenge.

There was no single all-powerful Potawatomi tribal chief. Thus, when French authorities required aid or support for some purpose, they had to appeal to various leaders of dodem and villages, singly or jointly. Similarly, their missionaries could target only individuals in their efforts at conversion. When a missionary eventually converted a wkama, only the members of that leader's clan might be affected.

It was the several Great Sea and Bear clans, together with their wives, who resettled in the St. Joseph Valley. Since these women were members of other clans, they helped maintain important ties to the rest of the tribe. Married women bound together the scattered clan memberships and the tribe as a whole.

The Potawatomi migrations continued for more than a century. Soon after the French made a lasting peace with the Iroquois in 1701, Antoine Cadillac, an administrator appointed by the governor of New France, established Fort Pontchartrain on the Detroit River. Many Potawatomi responded promptly to a French invitation to settle near this new stronghold. Later, others migrated south and west. Eventually, the Potawatomi's territory stretched from what is now Ohio west to the Mississippi River and south to the valleys of the Wabash and Illinois rivers. This remarkable achievement proved the wisdom of the leaders who had devised the tribe's basic policies back in the 1650s.

Some of the contents of the Sacred Bundle of the Human Clan. Top, left to right: *owl feathers, images of male and female clan ancestors, and a magic arrow.* Bottom, left to right: *a small wooden tablet with pictographs representing figures in songs; medicine pouches of woven beadwork.*

The Potawatomi achieved influential positions along all three major water routes connecting the French colonies with the interior.

To the French, settlement of their Indian allies in the area today known as Michigan, Illinois, Ohio, and Indiana helped create a barrier against British westward expansion. Indeed, this was the French imperial policy, designed to protect New France and the Louisiana colony. This policy inevitably led to great conflict.

For the Potawatomi, territorial expansion served their own purposes. It helped them solve problems that arose because of increased population, such as villages that had become too large for local resources. As the Potawatomi villages grew larger, there were more internal controversies, particularly between elder and younger generations.

The Potawatomi and the French were vastly different in their political arrangements. The former kept the peace and made decisions by consent and consensus. The latter relied on powerful authority and barely controlled competition.

When the French fought to defend their North American colonies against the British, the Potawatomi were prominent allies. In the French and Indian War of 1754 to 1763 they traveled widely and had many adventures. In nearly every year of that war, substantial raiding parties of Potawatomi were away from their homes for long periods, attacking English settlements from New York to Virginia, defending French Canada, or warring against the Chickasaw, Cherokee, and other tribes in the southeast allied with the English. In one of these battles the Potawatomi almost caused a dramatic alteration in the course of American history.

In the spring of 1755 the British assembled a large army under Major General Edward Braddock. Braddock led his regular troops and colonial militia northwest from Virginia to destroy French forts on the Ohio River. His guide and adviser, commanding 450 Virginia militia, was a young colonel, George Washington.

On June 8 the British were approaching Fort Duquesne in western Pennsylvania, the site of present-day

The Sacred Bundle of the Warrior Clan. Top: *feather shoulder drape and lance ornament.* Bottom: *magic miniature bow and arrow, and prisoner ties (handcuffs) of Indian hemp.*

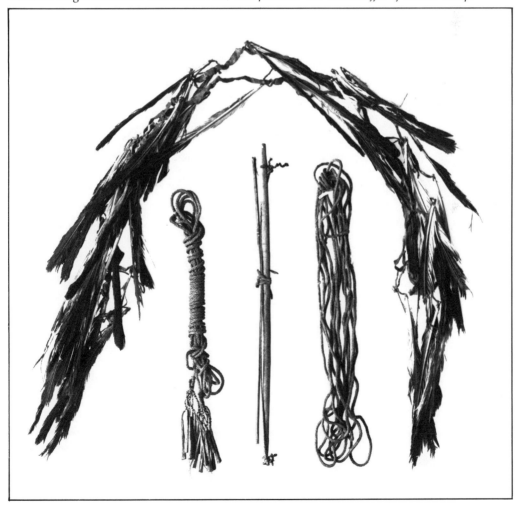

Pittsburgh. Seeing that the British were camped and on the alert, the Potawatomi war leaders persuaded the French not to attack. Instead, they planned to attack the British troops the next day while they were on the move, stretched out in mile-long files along a narrow, forest-shrouded trail.

Their surprise attack was a complete success. Colonel Washington tried to rally the demoralized forces and to counterattack in Indian style. But the British and colonial soldiers, unfamiliar with forest warfare, were defeated. They suffered nearly 1,000 dead and wounded out of the 1,500 on the trail that morning. The survivors fled, bearing the mortally wounded General Braddock with them. They abandoned most of their equipment, supplies, and hundreds of pack animals.

Washington barely escaped with his life. His equipment and clothing were shot through with a half-dozen musket balls. He learned a lifesaving military lesson from this disaster, one that he

General Braddock was fatally wounded, as were most of his troops, in battle near Fort Duquesne, now Pittsburgh. From the drawing by the French artist H. P. Philippoteaux.

(continued on page 47)

USEFUL AND BEAUTIFUL OBJECTS

In every century, wherever they lived, whatever else was going on in their world, the Potawatomi created beautiful objects. Although many of these are seen in museums today, they were made to be used as well as admired. These items had meaning: Their designs grew out of a rich store of shared symbols, a cultural vocabulary expressing the beliefs and values of their creators.

Natural materials—animal skins and bone, stones, wood and other plant parts—all went to create tools and sacred objects, clothing, and other necessities. Trade with Europeans and, later, Americans, brought new materials to the Potawatomi. From the 18th century on, their artisans used colored glass beads, silver and copper, manufactured cloth, and commercial yarn to create useful and beautiful objects. New design ideas, too, came from the Europeans. But even when the Potawatomi took ideas and materials from others, they made them serve their own needs and reflect their own values.

All these works are storehouses of information about Potawatomi life and culture. Although it may be difficult for us to decipher their symbols, we can all appreciate the knowledge that made these objects meaningful, and the skills that made them beautiful.

A medicine bag made from an otter's skin with porcupine quill decoration on the tail. A woman did the quillwork on this bag, but a man killed the animal, prepared its skin, and selected the sacred objects to go in it.

Because they were a mobile people, the Potawatomi needed containers of many kinds and sizes to carry food, sacred medicine, powder and gunshot, paints, and many other essentials. Their containers had to be flexible enough to be carried on the backs of humans or horses. Twined bags made of various natural fibers were the billfolds, briefcases, and bedrolls, the garment bags and diplomatic pouches of the Potawatomi. Bags were almost never purely utilitarian; colorful geometric designs added the joy of seeing them to their practical value. Bags were usually made from rushes, dried grasses, and other plant materials, used in their natural colors or dyed. Horsehair and other animal fibers were sometimes used as well.

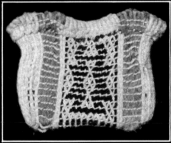

The two bags at left are fairly large, 18 to 20 inches wide and about 15 to 18 inches high. The bags above are purses, small containers for carrying personal items, only 2-1/2 to 5 inches wide and 2 to 4 inches high.

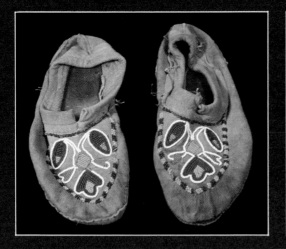
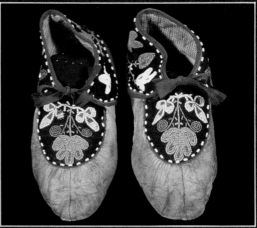

Moccasins like these were worn on ceremonial occasions, not every day. The beaded flower decorations were inspired by the designs on French textiles, modified to fit Potawatomi ideas about good design. Each tribe had its own characteristic style of moccasin. Beadwork, like quillwork, was done by women. Even today, Potawatomi women are famed among American Indian artisans for their beadwork, needlework, and ribbon appliqué.

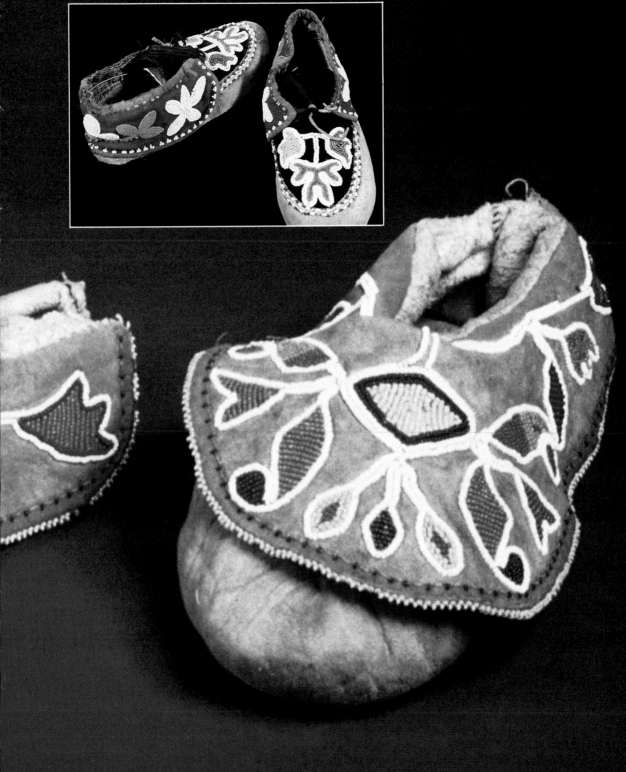

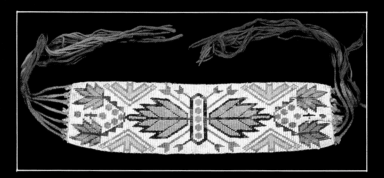

A beaded choker or neckband

A woman's beaded hair ornament with yarn and thimbles. The thimbles were like bells, ringing as the wearer moved her head.

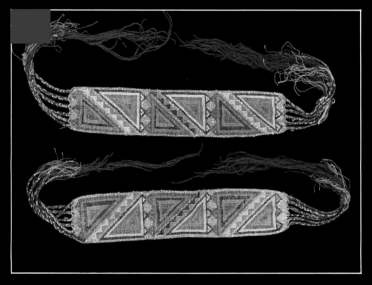

A pair of armbands. Geometric designs like this came directly from quillwork. When the Indians saw the colored glass beads of the European traders, they quickly adapted the techniques and designs of their quillwork to the new material.

A beaded choker or neckband

44

A heddle, used to raise and lower the fixed threads on a loom used to weave narrow bands of beads or yarn. The fixed threads or warp were alternately strung in the slots and through the holes in the heddle. The scalloped edge may have been inspired by a piece of European furniture.

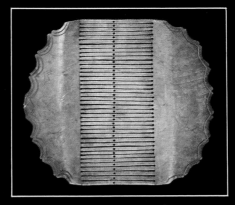

A woman's beaded bag or purse, woven in a geometric design derived from quillwork. Preparing quills for use was a time-consuming process. Indian women colored the quills by boiling them with berries, roots, or other plant parts. They flattened the quills while they were still wet and kept them damp and flexible as they worked. But beads could be used just as they came, brightly colored and ready to sew on or weave into clothing and ornaments.

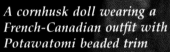

A cornhusk doll wearing a French-Canadian outfit with Potawatomi beaded trim

Armbands of tanned deerskin, with a beaded floral design and yarn edging

A paint bag in the style of miniature saddle bags. Because of its shape, this bag could be hung over a belt or carried. It would contain colored earths and other items used as face and body paint.

(continued from page 38)

himself would follow afterward and regularly give as advice to his own generals when sending them against British and Indian forces: "Beware of surprise!"

The Potawatomi celebrated their success while gathering up the spoils of victory. Among these were more than 200 horses, which they used to transport their booty. The horses formed the first herds the Potawatomi owned and caused a transportation revolution. The People had known of the advantages of horses, but never before had they owned more than a few at a time. Within a few years, most Potawatomi would forsake their bark canoes and rely on horses for transportation.

Horses were more rugged and reliable than the frail, fair-weather bark canoes. With them the Potawatomi could readily travel east and west, across the great north-south river valleys. They could travel to more places, in more months of the year. Soon they started hunting and raiding across the Mississippi River into Missouri and Iowa. By 1812 only those Potawatomi villages north of Milwaukee and a few on the St. Joseph River were still dependent on bark canoes. Most of the People relied on the horse and were now able to travel farther and faster than when their seasonal migrations had depended on canoe and foot.

Ultimately, though, the French and Indian War cost the Potawatomi dearly. The People had become accustomed to regular deliveries of tools, weapons, manufactured cloth and clothing, ammunition, and other goods from France. Although the French and their Indian allies had defeated Braddock and won other major land victories, the British ruled the seas. A blockade effectively halted shipping from France, cutting the Potawatomi off from their only regular source of trade goods. By 1763, when Great Britain finally conquered New France, the Potawatomi and other allied tribes were already impoverished.

The Potawatomi could hardly believe that the British had triumphed, since they themselves had experienced few defeats. They were cautious and suspicious when British emissaries first entered the western Great Lakes country to proclaim peace and assert their dominion over the tribes.

With the British victory came a flood of unregulated individual traders who soon penetrated Potawatomi lands and shoved aside their old French trading partners. The Potawatomi were angered. They were eager to trade, but many years of war had left them short of trapping equipment, and their century-old loyalty to the French lingered on. Their whole position had changed. No longer were they a most-favored tribe, whose services were treasured by a powerful European ally. Now they faced old enemies alone.

British authorities next committed a major diplomatic blunder. The new governor of Canada, Sir Jeffrey Amherst, had been ordered to reduce his administration's budget sharply. Among the major expenses he eliminated were the costs of the annual distribution of "Indian presents," goods

Chief Pontiac

and supplies that for a century had been paid out to the tribes in ritualized exchanges. Traditional forest diplomacy demanded balanced exchanges, material things flowing from Europeans to Indians, loyalty and fidelity going the other way. But to Governor Amherst, "Indian presents" were an expensive charity.

From the Indians' point of view, the English were not obeying the rules of the game. These powerful, wealthy foreigners came uninvited, claiming conquest of the region, asking for peace, friendship, and trade. Yet they did not bring rewards for the tribes' promises of alliance. Nothing of value could be seen in their hands. They needed a sharp lesson in tribal diplomacy. Open anger turned into organized rebellion.

This revolt of the tribes is known as Pontiac's War, after the great Ottawa war leader who was its best-known organizer and leader. This well-coordinated multitribal rebellion was spurred by the dream that the French would return to aid them. In May 1763, following carefully laid plans, the Potawatomi joined other western tribes in surprise attacks on every British post in the region. One by one the British positions fell, except for the two critical forts at Detroit and Fort Pitt (formerly Fort Duquesne; now Pittsburgh).

But the revolt was doomed. The French had neither plans nor means for aiding their old allies. The tribal allies, in turn, lacked both the tactical knowledge and the equipment to capture the major fortifications. Nor could they sustain a long siege and starve the defenders out, for they too soon became hungry. As summer turned into fall, small parties of Pontiac's part-time warriors broke away one at a time, returning to their villages to harvest crops and prepare for a winter hunt.

The British controlled shipping on the Great Lakes, which they used to dispatch relief to the besieged garrisons. Soon an invading British army pushed aside the scattered Indian defenders, one group after another. Not until October did the hard-pressed Pontiac learn why the French had not come to their aid: The French and British had made a firm peace eight months earlier. The siege at Detroit ended. The rebellion was over.

Pontiac's War was not a total defeat for the Indians, for the confederated

Pontiac and his men leaving the fort at Detroit. From a 19th-century painting by Frederic Remington.

tribes did achieve some of their aims. They taught the British authorities that the loyalty of the tribes had to be rewarded, regularly. There would be no peace on the frontier unless they periodically delivered to their new friends and allies the appropriate diplomatic symbols— supplies of food, arms, and equipment. This was an important lesson, for the British soon needed allies in the west. They were facing growing discord among their own colonial subjects on the Atlantic Coast to the east.

In London the British decided to issue a major policy statement intended to insure peaceful relations with the interior tribes. The Proclamation of 1763 created a boundary line along the crest of the Appalachian Mountains. West of that boundary was exclusively Indian Territory; no European settlers were to be allowed. All British colonial settlements were to be confined to the narrow strip of land east of the Appalachians. British authorities were trying to placate and control both the interior tribes and their colonial subjects on the Atlantic coast, but they could not please both.

The Proclamation of 1763 satisfied the Potawatomi and their allies and helped bring about 10 years of peace and prosperity. Its provisions were incorporated into the Quebec Act of 1774, which established a permanent British government in Canada. To the increasingly rebellious Americans in the east, the Quebec Act became one of the Crown's Intolerable Acts, because it counteracted their claims to western land. By setting up the western Indian Territory, the proclamation and its successor helped to bring about the American Revolution. ▲

The Potawatomi held on to much of their heritage even as they learned new ways from their new neighbors. Wapmimi (White Pigeon), who lives in Michigan, wears a Pan-Indian costume and mimics the movement of birds in his dancing.

COPING
WITH
AMERICANS

By 1776 some Potawatomi were being drawn into the American Revolution. Now they faced the threat of invasion by American settlers as a divided people. The vast expansion of their own territory made communication between the widely scattered villages difficult. Moreover, these distant Potawatomi communities had divergent interests.

When the war came, some villages sided with the British, others aided the rebels, and still others remained neutral. The Americans, traveling overland or down the Ohio River, came in large family groups and whole communities. These pioneers were intent on settling permanently on agricultural lands. Americans were a threat to the tribes because they were in direct competition for the resources of the same environments. At first they threatened mainly the easternmost Potawatomi.

Thus, in 1776, Potawatomi from the Detroit area supported the British, helping them by raiding the tiny American settlements on the Virginia-Kentucky frontier. But two years later, further west, other Potawatomi welcomed and aided American forces from Virginia, under George Rogers Clark, in their attacks on British posts in Illinois and Indiana. In 1781 came the high point in Potawatomi aid to the rebels. Sigenak (Blackbird), a Potawatomi leader well respected by both Clark and the Virginia patriot Patrick Henry, successfully led an attack against British positions on the St. Joseph River.

When peace came in 1783, representatives of the new United States believed they had, by conquest in a "just and lawful war," won sovereignty over the lands of Great Britain's Indian allies. Though ignored at the peace table, the Potawatomi and their neighbors did not believe they had been conquered.

Thus the stage was set for another prolonged three-way conflict; this time involving the British, the Great Lakes-Ohio Valley tribes, and the new, but weak, United States. The British were a continuing presence in the region

51

George Rogers Clark

north of the Great Lakes and the victorious Thirteen Colonies. Thirty years passed before Americans were at last able to exercise full control over the Great Lakes region, including all the lands occupied by the Potawatomi.

After 1783 the Potawatomi, increasingly united in their opposition to American expansion, attached themselves to the British. Although they won some important victories, in the end it was a futile effort, for the United States continued to expand in population, military power, and territory.

In 1784 the United States began negotiating treaties with the Indians, with the aim of acquiring their lands peacefully, by purchase. In 1787 the Congress passed an ordinance that created the

The signing of the Treaty of Paris in 1783, which ended the American Revolution. The United States was represented by (from left) Benjamin Franklin, John Jay, and John Adams.

Northwest Territory, which eventually became the states of Ohio (1803), Indiana (1816), Illinois (1818), Michigan (1837), Wisconsin (1848), and part of Minnesota (1858). These were years of dramatic changes in the lives of the Potawatomi and their tribal neighbors.

Soon after the Northwest Ordinance was approved, the tribes of the region organized as a confederacy and began defending their lands. Prompted and helped by their British allies, their aim was to keep the Americans from settling west and north of the Ohio River.

The frontier then exploded in a wave of violence. Twice the United States tried to impose a military solution. In the first effort, in 1790, 183 troops led by General Joseph Harmar were killed on the Maumee River in western Ohio. A year later, an American army under Arthur St. Clair, governor of the Northwest Territory, was almost totally destroyed in the same region. The western frontier was now defenseless.

President George Washington recognized that these defeats were due to inexperienced leaders and untrained troops. For the next action, he chose General Anthony Wayne, one of the most successful of his Revolutionary War officers. Called "Mad Anthony" because of his exceptional courage in battle, General Wayne was also a cautious and creative military leader. He heeded President Washington's advice: Beware of surprise!

For two years Wayne recruited, trained, and equipped his forces. Fol-

Governor Arthur St. Clair

lowing the military system that was used successfully in ancient Rome, he reorganized his troops into self-sufficient "legions." Each legion was fully prepared to operate and fight on its own. He also built a string of well-fortified supply points northward into western Ohio, toward the center of the Indian defenses near Lake Erie.

At the same time, President Washington's envoys worked at negotiating a settlement to the conflict. Only when the president determined that this diplomatic effort could not succeed did he authorize a general attack by Wayne's now well-trained legions.

The decisive moment came in mid-August, 1794. The Potawatomi and their allies, 2,000 warriors strong, were concentrated at a place called Fallen

"Mad Anthony" Wayne

Timbers, near modern Toledo. General Wayne did not attack hastily. Instead, knowing that the warriors would prepare for battle by fasting to cleanse themselves spiritually, he tricked them into believing he would assault their position days earlier than he actually intended.

Only when he learned that most of the hungry warriors had departed did he unleash his army. After a sharp skirmish, the few remaining Indians broke and retreated. Expecting to receive support from the British garrison at Fort Miami, they assembled there and called for help, but the British commander was under strict orders to avoid battle with Americans. Rebuffed and demoralized, the Potawatomi and their allies fled.

Abandoned by their British allies, the tribes of the western confederacy faced the Americans alone. In 1795 they made peace in a great treaty council at Fort Greenville, Indiana. General Wayne, now a soldier-diplomat, conducted the negotiation.

Wayne presented a new American position regarding Indian rights to land. The United States no longer claimed the land by right of conquest. Potawatomi and other Indian negotiators found this surprisingly generous, for they fully appreciated that they had been decisively defeated.

Instead, the Americans sought peace, acknowledging that the Indians had the right to occupy and exploit their lands until the land was purchased by treaty with the United States. At Greenville peace was declared, and large tracts of Indian land in Ohio and Indiana were sold to the United States.

All the Indian leaders participating in this momentous occasion understood that it was a time of transition. They now occupied lands subject to American authority, increasingly populated by American settlers.

In the following years, American policies for dealing with Indians were often based on misconceptions. Moreover, such policies changed often and were never consistently applied. One popular stereotype held that "the Indian" was a "savage hunter." Many influential Americans were convinced that as American farm settlements increased, wild game would disappear and the "savage hunters" would simply fade away.

Such stereotypes ignored important facts. The Potawatomi and their neighbors, like frontier Americans, were farmers, growing much the same crops and hunting to supplement their food supply. As Americans became more numerous, they competed with Potawatomi for the same resources—farmlands and game animals—in the same

environments. Moreover, as the forests were cleared and fields planted with corn, wheat, and alfalfa, game did not disappear. Instead, deer increased almost as rapidly as rabbits.

Americans also had little faith in the ability of Indians to change their customs. They ignored the fact that many Potawatomi desired to remain where they were, in their old locations, accommodating themselves to their new neighbors. The root of the problem was clear: The Potawatomi were tolerant of

Horticulture was traditionally women's work among the Potawatomi. The women in the background are gathering crops and hoeing. The woman in the foreground is shucking corn, putting the husks into one basket and the ears into another.

The Shawnee chief Tecumseh, a military and diplomatic leader, shown here in Indian dress, allied the Indians with the British.

Tecumseh, here dressed as a British officer, forced the British to stand and fight against the Americans in 1813.

cultural differences, while the Americans were not.

Of all American policies, it was the treaty system that affected the People the most. Treaties were formal contractual agreements, negotiated between American officials and Potawatomi leaders who represented various villages and clans. As Americans began buying large pieces of the Potawatomi tribal estate, the negotiations further divided the already scattered villages of this tribe.

But Potawatomi leaders proved extraordinarily astute in their treaty dealings. They had nearly a century and a half of experience in dickering with representatives of European powers. They

had, moreover, only recently acquired the huge territory that the Americans now coveted.

When they wanted to, the Potawatomi could stand together and present a united front. The Chicago trader John Kinzie commented on this attitude in 1819. He reported that although Potawatomi villages were widely scattered, each with its own independent leaders, those leaders were "perfectly republican & will not acknowledge anything *well done*, which is not done by a whole or a majority of them."

Thus, Americans found it easier to deal with smaller groups, to divide them in order to dispossess them of their lands. This policy increased the number of treaties negotiated and signed by the Potawatomi. However, the Potawatomi themselves saw opportunities in such negotiations. On several occasions they intruded themselves into negotiations with other tribes, demanding a share of the spoils, and threatening violence if they were not paid for lands where they had no claims.

The rapid loss of lands through treaties and the booming American population in their old territory soon led to new warfare. By 1805 some Potawatomi and nearby Indians began to make small-scale raids on settlers, traders, and travelers. These were unorganized acts of violence and protest, lacking leadership and widely accepted goals.

Leadership and a new philosophy of opposition to American expansion were provided by two remarkable brothers of the Shawnee tribe, starting in 1807. These were Tecumseh and Tenskwatawa, the latter also known as the Shawnee Prophet. Tecumseh provided the diplomatic and military leadership, while the Prophet contributed a religiously inspired vision of a new way to this new political power.

The new way, which President Thomas Jefferson called the Prophet's "budget of reform," called for steadfast, organized intertribal opposition to American expansion. The Shawnee brothers also preached rejection of American technology in an effort to make the tribes more economically independent. Their vision of an Indian utopia did not appeal to all Indians, but

Tenskwatawa, the Shawnee Prophet and brother of Tecumseh, who preached a vision of a new way of life to the Indians.

many younger Potawatomi became fervent converts.

When the British learned of Tenskwatawa's leadership and appeal, they embraced him and began using him for their own purposes. Then, in late 1811, another full-blown Indian war erupted across the Great Lakes frontier. The following year this Indian war merged with the War of 1812 between the United States and Great Britain.

For the last time, the Potawatomi from northern Wisconsin to central Indiana were united against American expansion. Reunited with their old British allies as well, they tried to face their opponents and their problems together.

At first the Indians and the British had great success. One after another, American garrisons fell to their assaults. But elation over early victories at Mackinac Island, Green Bay, Fort Dearborn (at the site of present-day Chicago), and Detroit was short-lived.

The Americans soon reorganized and counterattacked. In September 1813 Oliver Hazard Perry, commander of the U.S. fleet, destroyed the British fleet on Lake Erie. Their position near

POTAWATOMI TERRITORY, AMERICAN WARS

Potawatomi tribal lands at their maximum extent, 1812
→ Directions of additional expansion and influence
▲ Defeat of Harmar's forces, October 1790
O Defeat of St. Clair's troops, November 1791
★ Victory for Wayne's legions, August 1794

When Potawatomi chiefs signed treaties, they often drew their clan symbols on the documents to indicate that they acted as clan representatives, not for themselves alone. These signatures from a British treaty of 1806 represent two branches of the Thunderbird Clan, probably Partridge (upper left) and Sea Gull (upper right); Sturgeon (lower left, chasing a sunfish); Turtle (center) represents the Great Sea Clan. At lower right is a European signature, X.

Detroit now undermined, the British and their Indian allies retreated eastward toward Toronto.

The reluctant British paused for battle only when Tecumseh shamed their officers into it, insisting that they stand and fight, not run. It was his final battle, and the end of the western confederacy of Indians. At Moraviantown, on the Thames River in Ontario, just north of Lake Erie, on October 5, 1813, Tecumseh was killed by the Kentucky cavalry. With his death ended Potawatomi hopes of resisting American expansion.

The last attempt of the Potawatomi and their allies to act in tribal concert had failed. Never again would the People make war against the United States. In the aftermath of the War of 1812, the Potawatomi lost all of their remaining lands in the Northwest Territory. As a result they became even more divided and separated. Beginning in the late 1820s, a majority of them mounted their horses or launched their canoes for the fourth and last leg of their Great Lakes odyssey. When this last set of migrations finally ended, late in the 19th century, their descendants would be more scattered than ever before. ▲

In the 19th century, Potawatomi women decorated their shawls, wrap skirts, and leggings with designs cut from colored silk ribbons. They wore jewelry of silver as well as traditional bead and bone necklaces and beaded sashes.

A TIME
FOR
RESERVATIONS

Between 1789 and 1867 the Potawatomi negotiated nearly 60 treaties to sell off their land, parcel by parcel. This was almost twice as many treaties as any other single tribe. As the Potawatomi sold off choice areas by treaty, they sometimes were given reservations to live on. Reservations were tracts of land set aside by the U.S. government for the exclusive use of the Indians.

The Potawatomi had a variety of reasons for negotiating so many treaties. Lewis Cass, governor of the Michigan Territory in the 1820s, who knew the Potawatomi well, had one explanation: "The Indians always arrive at our treaty grounds poor and naked," he stated. "They expect to receive some part of the consideration at the moment of signing the treaty. This . . . furnishes the only motive for their attendance, and much the most powerful motive for their assent to the measures proposed to them."

Poverty was indeed a factor in the Potawatomi's willingness to sell land.

They had become dependent on manufactured goods, and as the fur trade declined in importance they no longer received enough income from that source to buy what they needed. They occupied so much land that many believed that they could sell part of it to obtain income for current and future expenses. They would sell a tract and then resettle on their remaining lands, depending on annuities (annual payments) from Americans for their land for their support. But as they sold more and more land, there was too little left for them to live on, and eventually the annuities expired. The People had exhausted their capital.

During the French era the Potawatomi had learned how to live on credit over the winter. In autumn a trader would advance a Potawatomi the ammunition, traps, and supplies needed for the winter hunt. The debt would be paid in the spring with furs taken the previous season. These were personal economic relationships and debts, one-

Governor Lewis Cass

control treaty negotiations. Most treaties provided for payment of substantial sums to these firms to reduce the Indians' debt. The U.S. government acted as a collection agency.

The United States itself profited from such dealings. The amount paid per acre for Indian land was far less than the price when the same land was later sold to settlers through government land offices. Large profits flowed into the nation's treasury. Individual states also benefited, for the annuity payments were funded by the sale of state development bonds.

Overall, the business of Indian land treaties was a great money-raising operation. The traders, the federal government, and the states all profited. So did the marginal people, now known as "half-breeds," "mixed-bloods," or "Indians by blood." These were the children, grandchildren, and great-grandchildren of Potawatomi women by French, English, and American men. Most of them had become small-scale traders, and the People were indebted to them as well as to the large trading companies. Like the trading firms, they too demanded and received payments during treaty negotiations. In addition to cash rewards, they were commonly granted tracts of land, usually a section (640 acres) or a half-section each.

Already, by the 1820s, these marginals were numerous. Most Potawatomi treaties contained long lists of these marginals' names, along with the amounts paid them: Alex Laframbois's children—$1,200; Margaret Muller—

on-one between an individual Potawatomi and an individual trader. Under President Thomas Jefferson, American officials created a new form of indebtedness to encourage later sales of Indian land. Soon trading companies, not individuals, delivered large quantities of goods to entire communities. No longer could individual Potawatomi make repayment from the products of their own labor. Debts piled up. The trading companies and the federal government considered these to be "national" debts, owed communally by each Potawatomi village or band.

Because the only way to pay these large debts was to sell communally owned land, the trading firms came to

$200; Joseph Laughton—one section of land; Edward McCartney's wife—three sections. These sums may seem small, but at that time a carpenter earned about $300 a year, while small farmers rarely saw or used cash. The land grants were especially valuable, for the grantees selected choice tracts, which they quickly sold to American settlers.

Tenskwatawa and Tecumseh had seen that the marginals would be a threat to the welfare of Indian communities. One item in their "budget of reform" had called for all children and descendants of French, English, and American men to be sent away from native villages and returned to their fathers' home communities. Efforts to accomplish this failed. Instead, the influence of the marginals continued to grow.

Other Americans, individuals and institutions, also profited from the treaties, which provided money for the salaries of teachers, blacksmiths, carpenters, doctors, millers, and missionaries assigned to help the Potawatomi become "civilized." Indeed, several famous institutions were originally supported by Potawatomi land sales. Notre Dame University, for example, was established on land that had belonged to the Potawatomi and was founded for the purpose of "civilizing" them. The treaties signed by the Potawatomi required them to pay, from the sale of their lands, for their own cultural transformation. In the end, they actually received only a fraction of the modest sums paid by Americans for

Traders and trappers were frequently "mixed-bloods" or marginals, children of French fathers and Indian mothers.

each acre of their land that they sold.

To gain the benefits they saw in these treaties, many marginals started claiming to be Potawatomi. Some communities successfully resisted this intrusion, but others did not. In 1842, for example, old *Padegoshek* (Pile of Lead), elder chief of the Potawatomi bands then living in western Iowa, voiced the complaints of his villages about these marginals, who had followed them west. Writing to President John Tyler, Padegoshek complained: "Many of these half-breeds claim exemption from . . . your laws—professing to be *Indians*—and at other times claim the protection of them—because they are *whites*. These things they do as suits their convenience. We wish them placed on the same footing as white men."

Such protests went unheeded. Instead Americans favored the marginals over traditional Potawatomi. Soon the marginals monopolized much of the resources allocated to the Potawatomi. It was their children who enrolled in government boarding schools, they who got the few available salaried jobs, they who willingly cooperated with large traders and Indian agents. Eventually the marginals won control of the business affairs of several Potawatomi communities. They transformed the social life of the Potawatomi—from within.

In this manner, by the late 19th century the Potawatomi's traditional view of the Good Life had changed radically. Once they had stressed economic and political equality, but the new social order was marked by political and economic inequality. In some reservation communities the marginals became an elite class, leaving the traditional Potawatomi poorer and more powerless than ever.

Meanwhile, Americans introduced a new policy. In 1830 Congress passed the Indian Removal Act. No longer could the Potawatomi remain on small reservations in the Great Lakes states. All eastern tribes, Potawatomi included, were pressed to sell their small remaining tracts so they could be resettled west of the Mississippi River in the new Indian Territory—what is now eastern Kansas and Oklahoma.

Some Potawatomi and other Indians had earlier abandoned their ancestral lands in the Lake Michigan area and moved west into what was then Spanish territory. After the Louisiana Purchase of 1803 they again came under American jurisdiction. The new Indian Territory was to be set aside for the exclusive, permanent use of emigrant Indians from the East, or so American authorities proclaimed.

Although the idea of Indian removal had occurred to Thomas Jefferson in 1803, it was President Andrew Jackson who made it into an effective national policy. The official, public justification was that Indian removal was a benevolent policy for the protection and welfare of Indians. In actuality, it was a policy of segregation, a plan to reduce tensions by separating Indians from American citizens.

Moving Indians westward benefited Americans in many ways. Millions of dollars flowed into the United States treasury from the sale of Indian lands. These profits paid for internal improvements such as new turnpikes and canals. Large sums went to private citizens through political patronage. The president, members of Congress, and other officials gave their supporters the valuable contracts and jobs that went with gathering up eastern Indians and moving them west of the Mississippi River.

The Indian Removal Act and the treaties written under its provisions promised the tribes that their new lands to the west would belong to them forever. Those who were reluctant to move west were grudgingly allowed to remain in the East, where they would

Removal of the Indiana Potawatomi in 1838. Forced west to Kansas, the Indians, on foot and horseback, are watched by Indiana citizens. The Wabash River, crossed by a timber bridge, is in the background. This scene was originally drawn by an eyewitness to the event, George Winter.

come under state laws and become citizens, with rights and obligations they had not previously had.

After 1830 most of the treaties signed by the Potawatomi dealt with their removal from the remnants of their old Great Lakes estate. Because the Potawatomi held widely different opinions about leaving their lands for the new Indian Territory, the removal policy left them more divided than ever before. In addition to geographic scattering, removal created great social problems. Their tribal organization had already started to break up; by 1848 they were no longer one people, of one mind, with a common culture and values.

American officials found it difficult to persuade or even force all Potawatomi to leave their old homes and resettle in Kansas. In the end, fewer than

half moved onto new reservations there. Many migrated willingly. These included several thousand independent people who, using their horses, had already been west of the Mississippi hunting and raiding other tribes. Other willing migrants included a few thousand Christianized Potawatomi, called the "Mission Bands," now dominated by an elite class of marginals, who saw more opportunities in the West.

But thousands more escaped removal entirely by going into Canada or northern Michigan and Wisconsin. Many others evaded removal and remained on or near their old lands. Again, the People demonstrated that they could turn American policy to their own uses.

The divisions caused by the removal policy for Potawatomi can be seen in a treaty negotiated in Chicago in September 1833. At stake were the last large tracts of land still owned by the Potawatomi in southwest Michigan, northern Illinois, and southern Wisconsin. Three opposing groups were involved. Potawatomi from the Lake Michigan shore north of Milwaukee arrived angry, loudly protesting the sale of their lands by the Menominee two years earlier. They had no intention of moving west, and never did so.

The Potawatomi from southern Wisconsin and Illinois, in contrast, did not object to removal. They were the most numerous and best organized group and sought the best possible terms and price for abandoning their lands. Their

Leopold Pokagon, Catholic Potawatomi leader

wkamek dominated the negotiations in Chicago. They sold all their remaining lands, agreeing in the treaty to abandon these and resettle in the West within three years after the treaty was ratified by the Senate.

The Potawatomi from Michigan arrived determined to hold on to their small reservations, but they bickered among themselves and soon divided. Only the Catholic Potawatomi of Michigan won the treaty-guaranteed right to remain in their area, thanks to the tough-minded, capable negotiating of their leader, Leopold Pokagon.

But words on paper are one thing. The real intentions of these Potawatomi, and their deeds, were a different matter. Within three years, most of those from Illinois and southern Wisconsin did act according to their agreement. They packed their belongings, saddled their horses, and journeyed west, settling briefly in western Missouri and then going on to Iowa. But some 2,000 others moved not west but northeast, into British territory along the Detroit River and the Lake Huron shore. The Pokagon band of Catholic Potawatomi in Michigan remained where they were, a right specified in their 1833 treaty, while the Mission Bands from Indiana moved directly into eastern Kansas.

Most of the northeast Wisconsin Potawatomi remained in their old homes along Lake Michigan for 20 years. Eventually, under pressure, they too moved elsewhere, but to northern Wisconsin, not Kansas. Similarly, sev-

NORTH DAKOTA

MINNESOTA

SOUTH DAKOTA

Missouri

NEBRASKA

IOWA

WISCONSIN

Mississippi River

L. Superior

ONTARIO

MICHIGAN

L. Michigan

L. Huron

L. Erie

United Bands Reserve

Prairie Band Reserve

River

Oregon Trail

Platte Purchase Reserve

Potawatomi National Reserve

Santa Fe Trail

Mission Band Reserve

KANSAS

INDIAN

TERRITORY

Independence

ILLINOIS

INDIANA

OHIO

MISSOURI

Potawatomi Reservations in the West, 1833–1861

Routes used by the Potawatomi in migrating to British Territory in the late 1830s and 1840s

Major land sales of the Potawatomi to 1837

eral thousand Michigan Potawatomi either moved into the northern part of that state or simply hid out until pressure for removal disappeared.

Thus, the fourth and last trek of the People's Great Lakes odyssey was caused by the removal policy. By 1848 their families, tribes, bands, and villages were widely scattered. But their migrations did not end then or there.

This was in part because of a faulty assumption in the Indian removal pol-

icy. In 1830 Americans assumed the United States would be a compact nation east of the Mississippi River, while the area to the west would remain a vast Indian Territory. They also believed that the United States had a God-given right to control the entire continent, a doctrine known as Manifest Destiny. As a result both of Manifest Destiny and the Mexican War, the United States would indeed extend across the continent within a decade.

Chemewse or Chief Johnny Green, wkama of the Buffalo Clan, and his family stayed in Iowa and joined the Fox Indians instead of moving to Kansas in 1847.

Within the continental United States, as one Methodist missionary remarked at the time, there was no place "this side of the Moon" that would safely be a large, permanent Indian Territory. When this became evident to American officials in the early 1850s, removal was abandoned and a new policy instituted. Thereafter, Indians could live on small reservations, but only temporarily. Their communal lands were to be subdivided and parceled out to individual families. Any surplus land granted to Indians was to be sold to American farmers.

This new policy aimed to bring Indians into the mainstream of American life as full, Christian citizens as quickly as possible. In part the policies reflected the opposition of many Americans to segregation, but the disposal of reservation land was more strongly supported by those who wanted Indian land for their own purposes.

The several thousand Potawatomi on the Kansas reservation found themselves still in the path leading to the American frontier. The Santa Fe Trail ran through their lands, and the Oregon Trail was not far away. A greater potential danger was that they occupied the best route for the transcontinental railroad then being planned and financed.

By 1861 these two forces combined. Some well-meaning Americans were determined to help the Potawatomi "improve" themselves, and railroad lobbyists were set to finance construction at the expense of the Indians. Despite the opposition of the stubborn conservative bands from Illinois and Wisconsin, the "national" reservation in Kansas, established in 1845, was broken up.

The Mission Bands favored the breakup of the reservation so that as individuals they could obtain land for farms and become citizens. Within a few years though, most had sold or otherwise lost their property. Now known as the Citizens Band, they were landless and impoverished. However, the conservative Potawatomi, now called the Prairie Band, held out. They

In 1842 the first covered wagon caravan traveled to the far west on the Oregon Trail, which passed near the Kansas reservation to which the Potawatomi had been removed.

were granted a smaller reservation carved out of a corner of the original, which they owned in common. Here the Prairie Band struggled for years to keep up a traditional way of life, practicing their old religion, hunting buffalo on the western plains, and warring with the Pawnee, Sioux, Cheyenne, and other tribes.

In the last years of the 19th century, the descendants of the ancient Neshnabek would experience a new and different kind of odyssey. No longer were their travels to be geographic. They were embarking on an endless social and cultural journey, one that continues today. They had to learn to live in a rapidly developing industrial nation. They had to cope, not simply with Americans, but with the modern world.

Anishnaabe, a member of the Deer Clan, studied at the University of Michigan in Ann Arbor and returned to serve her people of the Hannahville Band as a social worker.

PERSISTENCE
AND
REVITALIZATION

When the 19th century ended, the Potawatomi were widely separated, scattered across several states and Canada. Some lived in organized, land-owning communities under federal protection. Others, landless, existed as family groups or tiny bands in the nooks and crannies between American settlements. Many were no longer identified as Potawatomi; they had been assimilated (absorbed) into other Indian communities.

The Mission Band Potawatomi, who had become citizens in 1861 and were now known as the Citizens Band, soon reverted to legal Indian status. In 1867 they were awarded a small reservation in Oklahoma, then still Indian Territory. Meanwhile, the Prairie Band in Kansas remained stubbornly resistant to all efforts to "civilize" them. They held their 11-square-mile reservation in common as a tribe.

Other Potawatomi remained in Iowa, joining the Mesquakie (Fox) community in Marshall County and giving up their old identity. The Fox had avoided government control by purchasing their own land.

Three different groups lived in Wisconsin. Because all had sold their lands by the 1833 Chicago treaty, they had no recognized rights to land in that state. One of these groups, the Skunk Hill or Black River Band, was officially considered part of the Prairie Band in Kansas but preferred to live in Wisconsin.

In 1887 a larger Wisconsin group moved onto the Menominee Indian reservation and became legally Menominee, although they continued to speak the Potawatomi language. The smaller, third Wisconsin group, originally from the Lake Michigan shore, had settled in unoccupied parts of northern Wisconsin instead of moving west. There they became known as the "Strolling Potawatomi" because, landless, they constantly moved from place to place.

Michigan also sheltered numerous Potawatomi. During the 1830s and

1840s, some 1,500 had moved north to avoid removal. They settled among resident Ottawa and Ojibwa communities that still held rights to small tracts in the area. The Potawatomi were like chameleons, taking on a variety of protective ethnic colorations in order to live where they pleased.

This was true of the 2,000 Potawatomi who migrated into Canada in the same years. Although welcomed by British authorities, they had no treaty rights of their own. As Potawatomi they were not entitled to land, annuities, or services from the Canadian government. They soon settled among their old allies, the Ojibwa and Ottawa, who possessed small reservations.

Two small communities in southern Michigan further illustrate the variety of paths taken by the Potawatomi during the late 19th century. The Pokagon and the Nadowesipe (or Huron) Bands both successfully retained their Potawatomi identity as they coped with survival in a modernizing America. The first became Catholic, the latter Methodist, and both were soon English-speaking, landowning, taxpaying citizens of Michigan.

A Potawatomi family of northern Wisconsin, photographed in the 1930s. Family members wear traditional Indian as well as contemporary American clothing.

Descendants of the Potawatomi still live among the Ojibwa (Chippewa) of Canada, as the sign on this modern store on the Kettle Point Reserve indicates.

The Pokagon Band had the treaty right to remain in Michigan, but the Huron Band did not. Both, however, solidified their positions there by purchasing land. For the Pokagons this would create a problem because American inheritance law conflicted with their ideas of communal ownership. Title to their communal land was in the name of their leader, Leopold Pokagon. After he died the question of who should inherit caused grave disruption.

The Huron Band found an ingenious way to avoid such problems entirely. They persuaded the governor of Michigan to take perpetual custody of their land title on behalf of the community, thus creating a state-protected reservation.

Throughout the 19th century Americans believed that the Potawatomi and other peoples could not be both Indian and American. Americans of that time understood being Indian to mean be-

longing to a tribal organization, owning land in common, practicing "heathen" religions, speaking an alien language, and living apart from other Americans. The Pokagon and Huron Bands showed how false such assumptions were. The members of these bands became responsible citizens of Michigan, literate in English, Christians, and—the most powerful symbol of all—taxpayers. Yet, while living like other citizens and mingling daily with them, they remained Potawatomi.

But the very definition of who was a Potawatomi was changing rapidly. Until the 1820s, the People themselves had defined their own identity. Being Potawatomi required having a father who was a member of a clan. Children of Potawatomi parents became Potawatomi themselves by learning the traditional language and culture. Remaining Potawatomi obliged an adult to lead a proper life by traditional standards, contributing to the welfare of the family, clan, and community. By the end of the century, much of this definition of who was a legitimate Potawatomi would change.

A large part of this change came from outside. Americans and Canadians, for example, imposed their own legal definitions of being Potawatomi on the People. American ways of defining "Indianness" were and still are based on confused notions about race or "blood." According to Americans, a person who had even a distant relationship to a Potawatomi ancestor, no matter how little the "degree of blood," was still considered an Indian. This is a racist definition, based on biological myth, since there is no such thing as Indian or any other kind of "racial blood."

At the same time, many individuals and families who did not meet the traditional identity requirements of the Potawatomi clamored for recognition and acceptance within the community. From time to time numerous Americans decided there were advantages to being considered Indian, and many got themselves recognized as Potawatomi by various devices. One way was to claim adoption into a Potawatomi community. Another was intermarriage. During the mid-1800s, for example, some American men obtained Potawatomi rights by marrying a Potawatomi woman. Others simply invented Potawatomi ancestors, redrawing their family trees to suit their purposes. Sometimes all that was required was a position of power. In the 1890s, for in-

stance, a Kansas Indian agent wrote the names of his wife and children onto the official tribal roll, and their descendants have been listed as Potawatomi ever since.

A new government policy made it advantageous for many Americans to become Potawatomi. In 1887 the United States began a major effort to eliminate tribally owned reservations and to assimilate Indians into American life. The General Allotment Act provided a legal basis for the government to break up communal ownership of reservations and eliminate tribal organizations. The intention was for all Indians to become landowning, taxpaying citizens, so that the United States would no longer have to recognize or deal with tribal governments. This was to be accomplished by allotting (giving title to) farmsteads, taken from reservation land, to individuals.

The Prairie Band, which had held on to its diminished tribal reservation in 1861, strongly opposed the allotment policy. Under the leadership of an unusually outspoken leader, *Wakwaboshkok* (Roily Water), the band members stuck together, flatly refusing to accept individual allotments. Roily Water and several others were thrown into the military prison at Fort Riley, Kansas, for leading demonstrations, but the Prairie Band persisted in its opposition.

To break down this resistance, American authorities started awarding choice 180-acre allotments from the band's reservation to other individuals. People of obscure ancestry, among them the Indian agent and his family,

Wakwaboshkok (Roily Water), photographed in 1895. Called the "Gentil Brave" by some Americans, he led peaceful demonstrations protesting the General Allotment Act.

saw an opportunity for substantial profit. Under the pressure of having their land given away to others, the Prairie Band gave up. Finally the reservation was fully allotted, and within 30 years the People of the Prairie Band were nearly landless.

Every time a valuable resource, treaty money, or government service was made available to a Potawatomi community, outsiders tried to lay hands on these windfalls. The large sums available during the treaty era had attracted traders, the marginal "mixed-bloods," and many others. Many marginals had followed the Potawatomi west to the Kansas reservation, where they persuaded American officials to accept them as legitimate Potawatomi. They soon came to dominate the affairs of some communities.

The Mission-Citizens Band came under the domination of marginals by the 1860s. Even at that time many of their "chiefs" bore such non-Indian names as Joseph Napoleon Bourassa, Anthony Navarre, Perish Le Clere, and Claude La Framboise. These were the grandsons and great-grandsons of the old French traders, who continued their families' traditions of making careers among the genuine Potawatomi and extracting profits from their resources. The Prairie Band would not be dominated by marginals for another century.

Other Potawatomi communities managed to avoid such interference. Those who resettled in Canada left behind the marginals who had been associated with them in earlier years. They were aided by the Canadian law defining Indian status, which effectively blocked the marginals' attempts to obtain band resources. For different reasons, the Strolling Potawatomi of northern Wisconsin also experienced little interference. Landless, lacking even annuity payments, nearly impov- erished, they had nothing of value to attract the marginals.

From time to time the tiny Pokagon Band of southern Michigan attracted outsiders wanting to share in what seemed to be a bonanza. Three times in the last half of the 19th century, the Pokagons successfully lobbied in Washington for payments of debts owed them by the United States. Each time some marginals showed up to claim their shares of the fund. The last time was in 1895. The resulting confusion led the Commissioner of Indian Affairs to dispatch two special agents to investigate in 1895 and 1896.

Among the claimants were several thousand descendants of those Potawatomi who had fled to northern Michigan in the removal era. Their claims were excluded by the investigators because only the Pokagons had a treaty-guaranteed right to remain in Michigan, and only they had not been paid the

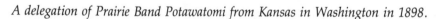

A delegation of Prairie Band Potawatomi from Kansas in Washington in 1898.

annuities due them. Those who had gone north had for years been obtaining benefits as Ottowa or Ojibwa. They could not now also claim to be Potawatomi.

One typical case was that of Alex Beaubien, from an old Chicago family, who claimed that he had a Potawatomi great-grandmother. After investigation, Special Agent M. D. Shelby rejected his claim. If Beaubien was an Indian, as he claimed, Shelby noted, "it was a fact he had carefully kept secret from his neighbors."

The leaders of the Pokagon Band, who worked hard for more than 50 years to win this case, were much annoyed by all these latecomers. They coined a new English word, in common use among them since, to mark such behavior. It is "meandom," signifying "mean" in the sense of selfish or greedy. "That's meandom for you," they say, pointing to strangers who show up wanting a share of the band's resources.

The Pokagons pioneered in using attorneys to serve their interests, and by the end of the 19th century most other Potawatomi communities were being represented by private lawyers. Generally, these legal firms went to the federal courts on behalf of their clients, seeking payments for injustices or failure to carry out the provisions of treaties.

In the late 19th century the more traditional Potawatomi found other ways to defend themselves and to improve their lives. Among these were new forms of magic and religion. In 1876 the Strolling Potawatomi and the Ojibwa of northern Wisconsin began to follow a new religion. Founded by a Dakota (Sioux) woman who came to them, it made marvelous promises. *Wananikwe* (Stranger Woman) was the only American Indian woman ever to found a new religion, one obtained in a visionary experience.

To those who gathered to hear her message, Stranger Woman explained that she had been pursued by the United States cavalry. For four days and nights she escaped the soldiers by hiding beneath the waters of the Great Lake. When she emerged she saw Christ walking across the water toward her. He took her by the hand, led her safely and invisibly through the cavalry's camp, and then taught her the new way.

Wananikwe soon found many willing disciples from among the hard-pressed Potawatomi and Ojibwa. But these tough old men could not tolerate a religious leader who was a woman. Wananikwe soon disappeared and no one ever heard of her again. Her disciples, missionaries of a new faith, then set out to preach her message and to make new converts.

This new religion blended the ancient with the new. Its beliefs centered on a great Drum, called Our Grandfather and thought of as a powerful supernatural person. The Christ who had appeared to Wananikwe was, the converts believed, Wiske in one of his numerous guises. Wiske, Christ, Our

A sacred drum used in Dream Dance ceremonies.

Curtis Pequano, Staff Man of the Dream Dance religion, holds the sacred staff to demonstrate the dream of Stranger Woman. In her dream, Christ struck the sacred drum to give it manido, *spirit power.*

Grandfather, and the sacred Drum—all were one. With new songs, rituals, and promises, Wiske, Our Grandfather, had returned. Wiske would restore power to the People.

This new Indian religion, the Dream Dance, spread rapidly. At first its central promise was political. Wiske, the converts believed, had given them a powerful magical weapon that they could safely use against Americans. Once they had enough converts and allies, they needed only to beat the great Drum for four days and nights, chant the new songs, dance the new dances, and follow all the ritual prescriptions.

Suddenly all Americans would "fall paralyzed on the earth." Then the People would be able "to walk among them and knock them on the heads with their tomahawks."

This message, spread secretly by Wananikwe's disciples, called for a powerful new alliance. A great council of tribes, from Wisconsin through Iowa and Kansas to Oklahoma, then north to the Dakotas and back to Wisconsin, would be enlisted. The Potawatomi saw this alliance in terms of one of their traditional symbols, a magical net. In their mythology, a magical net helped them overwhelm their prey on hunting and fishing expeditions. With this new magical-political net, their new prey, Americans, could be overwhelmed.

For some years the disciples were successful, making many converts in Wisconsin and Iowa. When the disciples reached Kansas, in about 1880, the Kickapoo and the Prairie Band Potawatomi were quickly attracted. But when the Prairie Band believers tried to carry the Drum into Oklahoma, they failed. They could find no converts among the tribes there. The magical net and the political alliance remained incomplete.

New religions such as the Dream Dance are known as cultural revitalization movements. Dynamic movements like this may arise when a people's traditional way of life is not coping with the pressures of social change. The revitalization movement tries to give the people a new sense of power and a whole new way of life, since the current way is not solving current problems. Often such movements look back to an idealized period in the society's past. Wananikwe's disciples, the true believers of the Dream Dance, looked backward. They wanted to restore the lost power, the lost sense of worth, and the customs they had enjoyed two centuries earlier. The Dream Dance shows the deep sense of loss among these traditional Potawatomi, their great anger, and even their hatred. The disciples hoped, by magical means, to restore power to the powerless.

While some Potawatomi lobbied in Congress and others sought justice in the federal courts, these strongly traditional groups sought relief from their culture hero Wiske and their old faith. Of course, the magic they hoped for could not work. No matter how often or how many worshiped Our Grandfather, Americans would never fall helpless on the ground and disappear from the continent.

But true believers do not easily abandon their new faith, even if they experience failures. Instead, believers change the basic promises of the new religion. That is what the Kansas Potawatomi did. Still adhering to the Dream Dance, they came to believe their new rituals would keep them together as a distinctive people. And this is precisely what the Dream Dance does for them, even today. Four times each year, at the change of seasons, the faithful gather and renew their cultural identity.

At those times, the social order of the ancient Neshnabek village appears on the Kansas prairies and in northern Wisconsin. As Wiske taught in the beginning, Man takes his place and Woman hers. The Wkama oversees all but has little power. Messenger carries tobacco, spreads the word, and invites all. Speaker preaches what everyone approves. Clan leaders have their say. Pipeman lights and passes the Great Calumet for all to smoke. All feast on the good things brought by Woman. The model of the good life taught by Our Grandfather is there for all to see and follow, helping the Potawatomi persist as Neshnabek. ▲

An elder at a meeting of the Pokagon Council, helping to draft a constitution for the band. A religious as well as political leader of his people who played professional baseball and fought in World War II, he works in a factory and is a lead dancer at powwows.

THE
PEOPLE
TODAY

When the 20th century arrived, the descendants of the ancient Neshnabek were no longer one people with a common language, culture, and territory. Yet however mixed their ancestry and wherever they lived, they were still called Potawatomi.

Most local groups faced their problems separately and sought different solutions. The Strolling Potawatomi, for example, at last ceased their wanderings. In 1913 they were given reservation land in Forest County, Wisconsin. There they settled, finally, as an officially recognized Indian community, eligible for federal services.

By then the Prairie Band in Kansas had lost most of its land, a consequence of the General Allotment Act of 1887. No longer did the United States deal with them as a recognized tribe.

Most annuity income from 19th-century treaties had long since expired for all Potawatomi. Opportunities for subsisting through hunting and fishing had declined sharply. The buffalo that the Prairie Band had formerly exploited were long gone. In Wisconsin and Michigan the deer herds were greatly reduced as a result of commercial hunting for urban markets. Few Potawatomi had become self-supporting, independent farmers, which was the overly optimistic aim of the General Allotment Act. Everywhere growing poverty was the rule.

The People tried varied ways to survive. Many worked seasonally as migrant farm laborers. Some added to their diets what small game they could capture. Families often kept large gardens, still tilled by women, sometimes aided by a man behind a mule- or horse-drawn plow. More and more they began to find wage-paying work in industry, first at unskilled jobs, later at higher-paying skilled trades. In later generations a scant few would get the education needed to enter the professions. There are no rags-to-riches stories to be told of the Potawatomi in the early 20th century.

Many developed cottage industries, producing finished goods in their home for local markets. People in several communities, for instance, made baskets. The materials for making baskets were gathered by both men and women, but the actual plaiting was done by women. These baskets were purely utilitarian containers, of many shapes and sizes, not works of art to be looked at in museum cases or on a collector's shelf.

There were many buyers for these baskets. The great American throwaway habit had not yet begun. There were as yet no cheap plastic or even paper bags. In stores, goods and produce lay unwrapped in bins to be picked over. Shoppers brought their own containers to carry their purchases in, and these containers were made of natural materials.

In minor ways the Potawatomi began to share in the general prosperity of the 1920s. But during the Great Depression of the early 1930s they were among the poorest of the poor. Then, in the first term of President Franklin Roosevelt's administration, came new policies for Indians, starting an advance that continues to the present. Known in their communities as the "Indian New Deal," the policy was expressed in legislation called the Indian Reorganization Act (IRA) of 1934.

The IRA had several beneficial features so far as its supporters in Washington were concerned. Not all of the

An Indian delegation to Washington greets President Franklin D. Roosevelt and his wife Eleanor in 1936.

Potawatomi agreed. The loss of Indian land was halted, and efforts were made to acquire additional land for their use. Loan funds for economic development became available, along with new educational and health programs. The most significant provisions of the IRA permitted Indians to organize as self-governing corporations. Each Indian community had to vote on whether to accept the provisions of the IRA or not.

The various Potawatomi communities reacted to the Indian Reorganization Act in different ways. Some, such as the Forest County and the Citizens Bands, quickly voted to accept the IRA. They prepared constitutions, elected community governments, and began managing their affairs.

The Pokagon community in Michigan, long ignored by the government, was particularly eager to come under the Indian New Deal. Year after year, through the 1940s, their leaders petitioned Washington, lobbied their senators and representatives in Congress, and wrote letters to influential people pleading their case. Faced with a limited budget, however, the Commissioner of Indian Affairs, John Collier, decided the IRA could not be applied to small communities that had long lacked official recognition, such as the Pokagons.

Meanwhile, in Kansas the local Indian agent labored to persuade the Prairie Band to accept Indian reorganization. He ran headlong into a stubborn clique of rebellious young leaders who flatly refused to have anything to do with him, Commissioner Collier, or the IRA. Anything the agent proposed, they rejected. Every step he took, they thwarted.

These rebels were the children of the leaders whose opposition to the 19th century allotment policy had failed. Several years before the IRA, the rebels had written their own constitution and established a governing council to their taste. Blinded by a generation of anger, confident of their own ability to go it alone, they could see no benefit in the Indian New Deal for themselves or their community.

World War II temporarily ended the programs of the Indian New Deal. During the war years the Potawatomi enjoyed a prosperity they had not known for a generation. Many served in the armed services and fought overseas. Numerous others worked in war industries throughout the United States.

Under the postwar administration of President Dwight Eisenhower, the United States returned to a conservative approach to Indian affairs, the earlier policy of assimilation. Indian community development was, for a time, forgotten. Instead, reservations and their tribal governments were to be eliminated under a policy called "termination." The goal now was withdrawal of special treatment and privileges for Indians. The Prairie Band, now virtually landless, became a target for termination, but their rebel leaders blocked this as effectively as they had the IRA.

In 1954 Congress added to the termination policy a law setting up an Indian Claims Commission (ICC). This

THE POTAWATOMI POWWOW

In languages related to Potawatomi, *pauwau* means "he has revelations" and referred to a religious leader. Today "powwow" is used in English to mean a lively meeting or conference, perhaps a political convention. It has also become a widespread Indian event. Here is the story behind today's Potawatomi Powwows.

In 1905 the Indian agent for the Prairie Band decided to hold a fair to show that the Indians were now farmers, acceptable to the other citizens of Kansas. Similar fairs were being set up by other Indian agents, using the traditional American county fair as a model.

At the Kansas Potawatomi fair, those Indians who were least traditional in language and habits were the most visible. To the Indian agents, displays of Indianness were unwelcome relics of the past. But Indianness was what American audiences most wanted to see at a fair, not jams, fancy quilts, and hogs. When a few aging chiefs appeared wearing old costumes, they immediately became the center of attention. Part rodeo, part county fair, the Kansas Potawatomi fair attracted large crowds every year until 1929.

In 1956 the traditional leaders of the Prairie Band decided to revive the fair as an annual Potawatomi Powwow. Many western states with large Indian populations were also reviving the old fairs as Indian-sponsored powwows. So many were held every year that singers, drummers, and dancers went from one to another to perform. A national powwow organization was created to coordinate schedules and events.

This national powwow development reflects continued interest in things Indian by Americans, who are the largest part of the audience. It also represents a revitalization of local Indian communities, for which the powwows are sources of pride as well as income. Locally, the powwow asserts tribal or band identity. Regionally and nationally, the powwow has become part of the Pan-Indian movement, which proclaims Indian identity and unity.

The Prairie Band Powwow has a genuine Great Lakes emphasis. Many participants unpack family treasures, bringing forth items of apparel that are true heirlooms. The dancers and drummers often wear antique outfits of hide and fur, with shell, animal tooth, and bone ornaments. They may wear vests, leggings, and caps decorated with beadwork or dyed porcupine quills and flourish old war clubs, calumets, bird-bone whistles, and tomahawks. Some wear 18th-century silver ornaments, produced long ago in Canada near Montreal for the Indian trade.

At the powwow today, Potawatomi from many places come together for recreation, family reunions, and renewal of old ties. Notables are honored, celebrated, or remembered. The modern powwow also serves an economic function: Admission is charged, and funds are raised for tribal purposes. Individuals also earn income from the sale of crafts, souvenirs, and food as well as from game booths. There are highly competitive dance contests with prizes. But above all, the powwow is an opportunity for the People to assert publicly that they are Potawatomi.

More recently, the Pokagons, the Catholic Potawatomi of the St. Joseph River in Michigan and Indiana, have started their own powwow, held every Labor Day in South Bend, Indiana. This new powwow is particularly important to them because they are not yet officially recognized as a tribe by the federal government. They have no reservation land, and their members are widely scattered. The Pokagon Powwow proclaims their existence as an organized community, declaring for all to see that they are unmistakably Potawatomi and must be recognized as such.

was a new but temporary federal court with special responsibilities to hear and rule on all Indian land claims against the United States. By then hundreds of special claims had been presented to Congress, but few had been approved for hearings in the regular courts. These claims concerned injustices in the treaties and land sales of the 19th century. The effort made by the Pokagon to win their case in 1895 is an example of how complex and difficult it was for Indians to get a fair hearing for claims arising out of earlier treaties.

In setting up the ICC, Congress intended to pave the way for termination of the tribes by settling all outstanding complaints. However, the operations of the ICC had exactly the opposite effect. Many millions of dollars were at stake. Once more, the value of being Indian was enhanced. Leaders of both the organized and unorganized Potawatomi groups were soon spending a great deal of time and effort to develop and prosecute their claims. On the fringes of these communities, many people were looking closely at their family trees, hoping to find a reason to share in the bounty.

Because the Potawatomi had negotiated so many overlapping treaties for land in so many places, the claims they brought before the ICC were far more complicated than those brought by any others. Small, unrecognized groups like the Pokagon and the Huron Band, for instance, first needed to get official approval even to bring claims, which they did.

Some communities opposed the claims of others, and there was much controversy. Eventually the whole collection of claims was sorted out. Two opposing groups of Potawatomi emerged, each with its own attorneys. This conflict centered on the efforts of the Prairie and Citizens Bands to prevent those Potawatomi who had remained in Wisconsin and Michigan from receiving ICC awards. This argument was finally rejected by the federal courts. All Potawatomi communities were allowed to share in the proceeds.

The next controversy erupted over how the substantial money awards were to be distributed. How large a share would go to each community in Michigan, Kansas, Wisconsin, and Oklahoma? The huge Citizens Band of Oklahoma argued that the total award should be divided in proportion to the numbers in each group at the time of distribution. The Court of Appeals saw this as an injustice and ruled that the funds should be divided in proportion to the numbers of Potawatomi in each band when the treaties were signed.

Those Potawatomi communities that had adopted IRA constitutions had approved a variety of membership definitions. Generally, these required at least one Potawatomi great-grandparent, or one-fourth degree of "blood quantum," as this concept is generally expressed. To avoid having their money awards split up into too many and too small shares, these communities held to their strict definition of Potawatomi membership.

The Citizens Band, in contrast, approved a generous "descendancy" principle. Any person with a Potawatomi ancestor, however far in the past, was eligible for membership. Thus today there are many members of this Oklahoma band listed as having one two hundred and fifty-sixth (1/256) degree of Potawatomi "blood." This reached back nine generations, some 225 years, to a single Potawatomi great-great-great-great-great-great-grandparent.

The stubborn Prairie Band leaders, the now-aging rebels who had sought independence in the 1930s, refused to approve any legal definition at all. They preferred to make their own decisions independently on whatever basis they liked. Until then the Prairie Band had never counted more than 780 members. Now, in the 1960s, the rebels had tried to reduce the number of "true" Potawatomi to 204. This caused so much controversy that in 1967 the Commissioner of Indian Affairs had to step in. The old Prairie Band leaders were cast out of power, a new constitution approved, and a new government elected. Its members and voters were mainly outsiders, people who had been marginal to the reservation community. Overnight the Prairie Band population increased tenfold.

This represented a victory for the American racial definition of Indian-ness based on "blood." The elder Prairie Band leaders had failed in their efforts to restrict Potawatomi identity to those who spoke the language and practiced the old culture.

By then the threat of termination had ended, a result of yet another policy shift. The ICC, however, established to help eliminate reservations and tribal organizations, was still active and its effects lingered on. The practical result of the ICC was to increase interest in being Indian and enhance the value of being part of a recognized Indian community.

The new Indian policy of the 1960s was initiated near the end of President John F. Kennedy's administration and

A Kansas Potawatomi elder, photographed in front of her home in 1963.

James Wahbnosah, a Kansas Potawatomi ritual leader and elder in 1963.

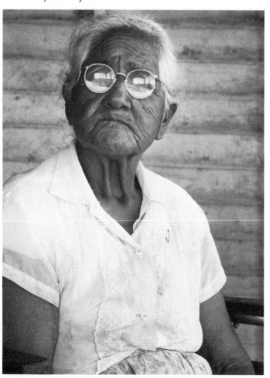

Potawatomi women, long accustomed to making baskets for everyday use, now weave finely crafted baskets of black ash splint to sell at powwows and galleries. Two elders of the Pokagon Band display their baskets at a recent powwow.

put into effect under President Lyndon B. Johnson. The policy now was to build up Indian communities, developing their resources, improving their economies, increasing the level of education, and generally enhancing the quality of Indian life. Nationwide, the various programs to improve the quality of life for other Americans were known as the War on Poverty. Like other Indians, the Potawatomi were eligible for all the special programs in this general attempt to uplift impoverished Americans as well as for others designed specifically for Native Americans.

Most Potawatomi eagerly embraced the War on Poverty and were soon beneficiaries of health, education, eco-nomic development, and many other government programs. Not so the old rebels of the Prairie Band reservation, who reacted to President Kennedy's policies as they had to those of President Roosevelt 30 years earlier. Independent as always, they again flatly rejected the idea of participating, turning away the grant funds available for improving services and life on the reservation. While other Potawatomi were inviting and providing hospitality to representatives of the Office of Economic Opportunity, these older Kansas leaders were driving them away.

These same years witnessed a general surge of interest in American ethnic groups, particularly in Indians. It was the decade not only of a War on Poverty but of battles for civil rights. The Indian version of the Civil Rights movement quickly involved many Potawatomi, among whom the traditional Prairie Band members were particularly militant. Some participated in the sit-ins and takeover attempts of the Red Power movement. Among the better known exploits were the 1971 occupation of Mount Rushmore, the Trail of Broken Treaties caravan to Washington and sit-in at the Bureau of Indian Affairs of 1972, and the demonstrations in 1973 at Wounded Knee, South Dakota, to commemorate a battle of 1890. But while the Indians' energies were engaged in such dramatic and emotional confrontations, they were doing little to cope with day-to-day problems on the reservation.

These episodes put Indian affairs on the television screen and on the front pages of newspapers and increased awareness of issues concerning the Indians. Efforts to upgrade the quality of life in Indian communities have continued. Education in particular is seen as a means of making broad improvements. Many colleges and universities developed Native American Studies programs. By the 1980s the numbers of Potawatomi finishing secondary education and college had increased substantially.

Such developments contained their share of irony. As late as the 1950s, culturally conservative Potawatomi communities resisted sending their children to school at all. Formal education in

Hundreds of Indians marched on Washington in 1972, blocking the entrance to and later sitting in at the offices of the Bureau of Indian Affairs.

American institutions, they believed, would negate their efforts to teach their language and traditions. By 1986 the leaders in these same communities were suing local school districts for not providing programs to allow their young people to graduate from high school. A new generation of leaders realized that an American education was the key to success in modern life.

Contemporary relationships between the People and Americans of European, African, and Asian heritage are as paradoxical as they were three centuries earlier. The wkamek who first invited Claude Allouez and Nicholas Perrot into their villages in the 17th century could already see some of the contradictions between their traditions and those of the alien French. At that time the Neshnabek were many, strong and influential, an independent people who protected their own frontiers. They, the grandchildren of Wiske, were one in language and culture.

Since then the Potawatomi have become few, weak, scattered, and dependent on outsiders. Individuals dissatisfied with decisions of Potawatomi councils about admitting them as members, for instance, now turn to the federal courts for redress. Without the special economic, legal, and educational programs available to them to-day, none of these communities could last for long.

There are today few Potawatomi who can trace their ancestry solely to those who lived in the villages on the shores of Mitchigami in 1634. All are the descendants of three centuries of intermarriage with French, English, Americans, others of European ancestry, other Indians, and sometimes peoples of African and Asian origin as well. Several thousand individuals carry identification cards certifying that they are recognized by some band and the United States as legal Potawatomi. There is no other visible way to determine their ancestry.

Yet today, too, there are hundreds of others who continue to speak the old language, behaving as closely to the old ways as they can, living isolated from other Americans. Although they may be poor in material goods, these traditional Potawatomi are rich in their Neshnabek heritage. In such families the elders on winter nights still gather young children around them, teaching as their ancestors have done all these many years:

> In the beginning there was no land, only water. Floating on this Great Sea was a birchbark canoe. In it, weeping, sat a man, Our Grandfather. He wept because he had no idea of his fate. . . .

BIBLIOGRAPHY

Bee, Robert L. "Potawatomi Peyotism: The Influence of Traditional Patterns." *Southwestern Journal of Anthropology,* Vol. 22 (1964): 194–205.

Clifton, James A. "Chicago, September 14, 1833: The Last Great Indian Treaty in the Old Northwest." *Chicago History* (Summer 1980).

———. "From Bark Canoes to Pony Herds: The Great Lakes Transportation Revolution, 1750–1775." *Henry Ford Museum and Greenfield Village Herald* (Winter 1986).

———. "Merchant, Soldier, Broker, Chief: A Corrected Obituary of Captain Billy Caldwell." *Journal of the Illinois State Historical Society* (Winter 1979): 185–210.

———. *A Place of Refuge for All Time: Migration of the American Potawatomi into Upper Canada.* Ottawa: National Museum of Man, 1975.

———. *The Pokagons, 1683–1983: Catholic Potawatomi of the St. Joseph River Valley.* Washington, D.C.: University Press of America, 1984.

———. "The Potawatomi." In Bruce Trigger (ed.), *Handbook of North American Indians,* Vol. 15, *Northeast.* Washington, D.C.: Smithsonian Institution, 1978.

———. *The Prairie People: Continuity and Change in Potawatomi Indian Culture.* Lawrence, KS.: University Press of Kansas, 1977.

Landes, Ruth. *The Prairie Potawatomi: Tradition and Ritual in the Twentieth Century.* Madison, WI: University of Wisconsin Press, 1970.

THE POTAWATOMI AT A GLANCE

COMMONLY CALLED   *Potawatomi*

OWN NAME   *Neshnabek*

TYPE OF SOCIETY   *tribal, multi-village*

TRADITIONAL ECONOMY   *mix of horticulture, hunting, fishing*

CULTURE AREA   *Northeast Woodlands, Great Lakes-Riverine Region*

LINGUISTIC FAMILY   *Central Algonquian*

FIRST EUROPEAN CONTACT   *Jean Nicolet, French, 1634, near Green Bay, Wisconsin*

HOMELAND AT FIRST CONTACT   *southwest Michigan*

TRADITIONAL POPULATION AT FIRST CONTACT   *2,500*

SELF-IDENTIFIED POPULATION TODAY   *over 22,000*

MODERN STATUS
Canada   *assimilated into other reservation communities.*
United States   *separate band reservations in Michigan, Wisconsin, Kansas, and Oklahoma; assimilated into other reservation communities in Michigan, Wisconsin, Iowa, and Kansas. Most self-identified "Potawatomi" have little association with tiny traditional reservation groups.*

GLOSSARY

Allotment A United States policy, applied nationwide from 1887, intended to assimilate Indians into the mainstream of American life by breaking up tribally owned reservations and tribal organizations. Each individual tribe member was given or "allotted" a share of land for private farming and became a citizen of the state.

assimilation Adoption by individuals of the customs of another society; a means by which the host society recruits new members. The United States, as well as most American Indian societies, gained new members in this fashion.

band The smallest, simplest type of politically independent society, usually a group of related persons, 300 or fewer, subsisting by foraging and occupying a specific territory.

clan A multigenerational group having a shared identity, organization, and property, based on belief in descent from a common ancestor. Because clan members consider themselves closely related, marriage within the clan is strictly prohibited. Potawatomi clans were based on descent through the male line.

creation or origin myth A sacred narrative that the people of a society believe explains the origins of the world, their own institutions, and their distinctive culture.

culture The knowledge a group has about its world, used to make sense of its experience and as a guide for all of its activities.

culture hero The central figure or figures in a creation myth. Wiske and Chipiyapos were the culture heroes of the Potawatomi.

cultural revitalization movement A system of new rituals that develops at a time of great cultural stress and disorganization, intended to improve conditions and bring about a new and more satisfying way of life.

descendency roll A membership list of a contemporary Indian organization that does not require a minimum degree of Indian ancestry. Such membership rules benefit marginals and increase the recognized "Indian" population.

dodem Potawatomi word for *clan*; also used to refer to a clan's symbol of identity and to the clan's members. This word came into the English language as "totem."

earth diver myth A type of origin myth featuring animals who swim beneath the surface of a vast original sea and bring up bits of dirt from which the culture hero fashions the Earth. Widespread in North America and other parts of the world.

foraging An economic system based on the collection of wild plant foods, animals, and fish; the most ancient of human ways of obtaining the necessities of life. Foragers are often called hunting and gathering societies.

horticulture The production of food by human muscle power and simple hand tools, used in planting and harvesting domesticated crops. Horticulture is commonly women's work. Agriculture, which requires the power of draft animals and larger tools such as plows, is usually men's work.

Indian Claims Commission (ICC) A special, temporary federal court set up in 1948 to settle all outstanding Indian land claims against the United States. The ICC generally had to decide whether a tribe had been underpaid for particular lands during the treaty era (before 1871) and how much additional payment was due.

Indian Reorganization Act Federal legislation of 1934 ending the allotment policy and providing for political and economic development of reservation communities.

linguistics The scientific study of the sounds, vocabulary, meanings, and grammar of languages.

Manido A complex Potawatomi word that can refer to spiritual power, excellence, a supernatural being, or a source of excellence. Also used to refer to a specific manifestation such as the guardian spirits that come to Potawatomi youth in their vision quest.

marginals People who identify with and live on the edges of two cultures and who move from one to the other depending on where they find the greatest rewards at any given time.

Métis French term for "mixed." Refers to the offspring of French men and Indian women.

Neshnabe, Neshnabek The term used by the Potawatomi for themselves; literal meaning is "True Human" or "True People." *Neshnabe* also means "a male."

patrilineal, patrilineality A principle of descent by which kinship is traced exclusively through male ancestors; basis for Potawatomi clan membership.

Potawatomi The name mistakenly given by the French to those who called themselves Neshnabek; supposedly meaning "People who make fire."

removal policy National policy of 1830 calling for the sale of all Indian land in the states and the migration of Indians from eastern and southern states to and resettlement in a segregated, exclusively Indian territory (Kansas and Oklahoma). Those Indians who remained in the east came under state laws.

reservation A tract of land set aside by treaty for the occupation and use of Indians. Some reservations were for entire tribes, many more for individuals and families.

sacred bundles Objects of great *manido* kept in a decorated animal skin and used in rituals. Bundles could be owned and used by clans or individuals.

subsistence economy The knowledge, skills, and tools used by a society to obtain food, clothing, and shelter.

treaty A contract negotiated between representatives of the United States (or Great Britain) and one or more Indian tribes. Treaties dealt with surrender of political independence, peaceful relations, land sales and payments for them, boundaries, and related matters.

tribe A type of society consisting of several or many separate communities united by kinship and such social units as clans, religious organizations, and economic and political institutions. Tribes generally share a common culture and language, are characterized by economic and political equality, and thus lack social classes and authoritative chiefs.

vision quest A ritual required of all adolescent Potawatomi boys (and permitted for some girls), involving long, lonely vigils out-of-doors without food or water. The goal was to have a dream or vision of a *Manido,* a spirit being who would become the person's protector and guardian.

wkama, wkamek Potawatomi word for leader, of which there were many kinds: *wkamek* of clans and villages, *wkamakwe* (leader of the women), *wabosowkama* (leader of the rabbits). Potawatomi wkamek were leaders but not authority figures.

ACKNOWLEDGMENTS

Cover: Photograph courtesy of the Cranbrook Institute of Science, Bloomfield Hills, Michigan.

Pages 12, 22, 32, 50, 55, 60, 70, 80, drawings by Michèle Gauthier. Published by Beaver Quill Studio, St. Joseph, Michigan; 14, 17, 24, 29 *top*, 31, 42–43, 46 *upper left*, photographs courtesy of the Museum of the American Indian, Heye Foundation; 15, 36, 37, 72, 78 *left*, Milwaukee Public Museum of Milwaukee County; 16, drawn from the original by Seth Eastman. From Schoolcraft, *History of the Indian Tribes of the United States*, pt. 3, p. 68. The Newberry Library; 18, 26, 38, 48, 49, 52 *top and bottom*, 53, 54, 56 *top left and right*, 62, 63, 69, The Bettmann Archive; 21, painting by E. M. Deming, The Bettmann Archive; 27 *top and left*, 29 *bottom*, 39, 40, 41, 42 *top left and right*, 43 *top left* 44, 45, 46, Cranbrook Institute of Science, Bloomfield Hills, Michigan; 30, photograph by Robert L. Bee; 57, Amon Carter Museum, Fort Worth, Texas; 59, 73, 78 *right*, 88 *bottom left and right*, photographs by the author; 65, Tippecanoe County Historical Association. Gift of Mrs. Cable G. Ball. Original sketch by George Winter; redrawn by Michèle Gauthier; 66, Northern Indiana Historical Society, South Bend, Indiana; 68, photograph by the Elliott Brothers, courtesy of the Bureau of American Ethnography, Smithsonian Institution, Washington, D.C.; 75, 76, photograph by DeLancey Gill, courtesy of the Bureau of American Ethnography, Smithsonian Institution, Washington, D.C.; 82, 90, UPI/Bettmann Newsphotos; 85 *bottom and inset*, 89, photographs by Barbara Paxson.

Maps (frontispiece, 25, 34, 58, 67, 87) by Gary Tong.

The Potawatomi of Kansas have offered me much hospitality and patience. Others, elsewhere, have done the same, welcoming me, my wife, my children, and my students. All of them have helped. I thank Faye and our Peggy, Peter, Caty, and Doug, who are children no more. I thank Bob Bee, Ann McElroy, Gary Gossen, and Barry Isaac, who are young students no more. Over the years, my anthropological and historical research were aided by grants from the National Science Foundation, the Wenner-Gren Foundation, the Canadian Ethnology Service, and the National Foundation for the Humanities. My gratitude goes to these fine organizations. Most of all I thank the People, from Parry Island, on the cold shores of Lake Huron, to Holton, Kansas. So far as I can tell, they will be Neshnabek for a long time to come.

James A. Clifton
Green Bay, Wisconsin
1987

JAMES A. CLIFTON is a cultural anthropologist and a leading authority on the ethnohistory of the Indians of the Great Lakes — Ohio Valley area. He is Frankenthal Professor of Anthropology and History at the University of Wisconsin, Green Bay, and previously taught at the Universities of Oregon, Colorado, and Kansas. He earned a Ph.B. at the University of Chicago and a Ph.D. at the University of Oregon. He was a merchant seaman in World War II and a U.S. Marine Corps infantry officer during the Korean War, when his interest in other cultures developed. His research has concerned the peoples of Micronesia, Chile, and the Indians of the United States and Canada, and he has done field research in Indian communities in Oregon, Colorado, Wisconsin, Kansas, and Canada. He has been a research consultant and expert witness in Indian treaty rights cases in the federal courts. Author of a dozen books and more than 160 articles and essays, he has a special interest in carrying the lessons of anthropology and of his research on Indians and other native peoples to general readers, especially young audiences.

———————————————

FRANK W. PORTER III, General Editor of INDIANS OF NORTH AMERICA, is Director of the Chelsea House Foundation for American Indian Studies. He holds an M.A. and Ph.D. from the University of Maryland, where he also earned his B.A. He has done extensive research concerning the Indians of Maryland and Delaware and is the author of numerous articles on their history, archaeology, geography, and ethnography. He was formerly Director of the Maryland Commission on Indian Affairs and American Indian Research and Resource Institute, Gettysburg, Pennsylvania, and he has received grants from the Delaware Humanities Forum, the Maryland Committee for the Humanities, the Ford Foundation, and the National Endowment for the Humanities, among others.

17.95